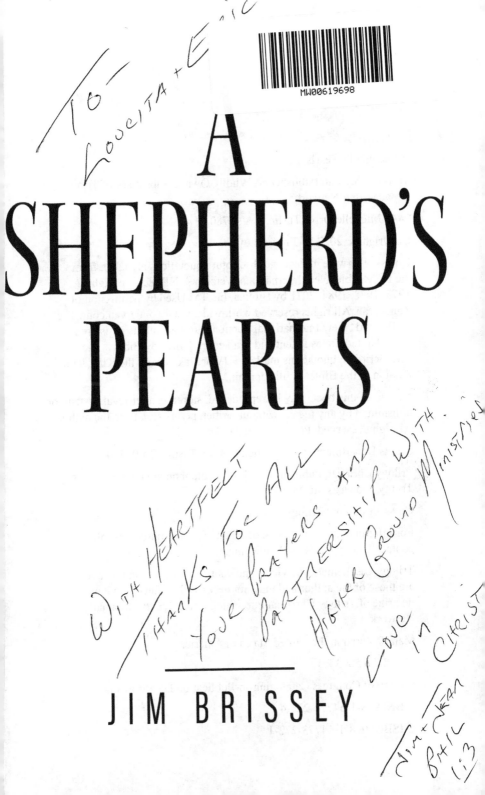

To Louella + Eric

# A SHEPHERD'S PEARLS

With Heartfelt Thanks for all your prayers and Partnership with Higher Ground Ministries

Love in Christ

Jim + Fran
B7416 1:3

## JIM BRISSEY

TRILOGY
PROFESSIONAL PUBLISHING MEETS POWERFUL PROMOTION

A wholly owned subsidary of TBN

A Shepherd's Pearls

Trilogy Christian Publishers A Wholly Owned Subsidary of Trinity Broadcasting Network

2442 Michelle Drive Tustin, CA 92780

Manufactured in the United States of America

10 9 8 7 6 5 4 3 2 1

Library of Congress Cataloging-in-Publication Data is available.

ISBN: 978-1-64773-271-4

E-ISBN: 978-1-64773-272-1

# FOREWORD
## by Gigi Graham

"Once again, my friend Jim Brissey has authored a book that is wonderful, encouraging, warm and a personal testimony to the fact that God uses everyday experiences and encounters not only to bring us closer to Him, but to further His kingdom.

Through these stories (pearls) this shepherd shares, we learn that if we give ourselves to Him, God can use any of us for His glory and give us a life filled with blessings and joy.

Thank you, Jim, for sharing your precious pearls with us."

# DEDICATION:

*"A Shepherd's Pearls" is dedicated to my
family who I love with all my heart.*

# ENDORSEMENTS
## for A Shepherd's Pearls:

I first met Pastor Jim Brissey at Lighthouse Via de Cristo #12. Jim was the spiritual director, and I was one of many candidates. He likes to call me his "Barnabas", but I consider myself his "Timothy". Although the last twenty years our steps have been numbered with miles in between, we have remained close and united as brothers in Christ. Jim has been my good shepherd, and his friendship, love and ministry have enriched my life and my walk with the Lord in ways that words cannot express. His ministry is real life, church-led and family centered. I pray as you read Jim's testimony and read God's Word as shared through the many stories in this book, the Holy Spirit will reveal to you pearls of right standing and transformation which will deepen your faith and love of Jesus.

**William T. Morgan, MD**
*CEO of Copiah County Medical Center*

Jim is my brother in Christ and partner in ministry for more than 25 years. He continues to inspire me with the authenticity and transparency of his walk with the Lord. When I could no longer speak, preach and sometimes think clearly following a health crisis that left me disabled, Jim has been there. At my lowest and loneliest, he was the one who showed up. His servant leadership in various ministries and outreach to the poor, imprisoned and forgotten demonstrates what I believe is his core mission: "Your kingdom come, Your will be done, on earth as it is in heaven". Enjoy this shepherd's pearls!

**Pastor John Barham**
*Methodist Pastor for 40 years*

I met Pastor Jim in 1995 while I was serving 5 life sentences at Zephyrhills C.I. While incarcerated, I was graced to serve on 36 Kairos weekends. After graduating from Higher Ground School of Ministry I served as administrator for 6 cycles of the 67 class HGSM curriculum at Putnam Prison, assisting more than 50 men to graduate. I was released from prison after serving 27 years 111 days. I am now serving as a Shelter Coordinator at The Bridge Shelter in Deland and as a Deacon in my church.

**Deacon Thomas Duckett**
*Deland, Florida*

Jim Brissey's book, "A Shepherd's Pearls", is the splendid spiritual autobiography of a man of deep faith. The book will warm your heart with stories of his spiritual journey of religion to being born again and on to works of love and service. This book will make you laugh, wince, and at times put a tear in your eyes. A message from the head reaches the head, while a message from the heart reaches the heart. This book is truly a full heartfelt message to any reader. Knowing Jim and sharing prison ministry with him for more than 20 years, I have personally seen him live out his words in action over and over again.

**Rev. David K. Miller**
*Former Sr. Chaplain Putnam Prison*

I met Pastors Jim and Jean and the Higher Ground team in the 90's at Putnam Correctional Institution. That fiery-eyed preacher set the chapel on fire! I knew then there was something special about this ministry. It was unknown to me, at the time, they would become my spiritual mentors. Throughout the twenty plus years I have been honored to serve with Higher Ground Ministries, we've seen thousands of souls touched and saved from the cells of Death Row to the beaches of Daytona.

**James "Gator" Leggett**
*Guest on The 700 Club*

# TABLE OF CONTENTS

Introduction. . . . . . . . . . . . . . . . . . . . . . . . . . . . . . . . . . . . . . . 13

Chapter One: How I Marvel . . . . . . . . . . . . . . . . . . . . . . 17

Chapter Two: The Broken Years. . . . . . . . . . . . . . . . . . 25

Chapter Three: Pressing On . . . . . . . . . . . . . . . . . . . . . . 39

Chapter Four: Come, Holy Spirit . . . . . . . . . . . . . . . . . 47

Chapter Five: Kairos—God's Special Time . . . . . . . . . . 59

Chapter Six: Ten Thousand Counselors . . . . . . . . . . . . 65

Chapter Seven: Purposeful Grace . . . . . . . . . . . . . . . . . 73

Chapter Eight: Sweet Spot of Grace . . . . . . . . . . . . . . . 85

Chapter Nine: Life-Changing Kephale . . . . . . . . . . . . . 95

Chapter Ten: Sensing God's Pleasure . . . . . . . . . . . . . 107

Chapter Eleven: God Makes a Way . . . . . . . . . . . . . . . 117

Chapter Twelve: A Blasted Protestant. . . . . . . . . . . . . 127

Chapter Thirteen: Accountability or Pain? . . . . . . . . . . 139

Chapter Fourteen: Life and Death. . . . . . . . . . . . . . . . 147

Chapter Fifteen: Grace for the Humble . . . . . . . . . . . . 159

Chapter Sixteen: A Firehouse Revisited . . . . . . . . . . . . 171

Chapter Seventeen: A Bad Question. . . . . . . . . . . . . . 185

Chapter Eighteen: Adventure and Discovery . . . . . . . . 197

Chapter Nineteen: The King's Party . . . . . . . . . . . . . . 211

Chapter Twenty: Red Man, White Man . . . . . . . . . . . . 221

Chapter Twenty-One: Unexpected Blessings . . . . . . . . 231

Chapter Twenty-Two: Pastors Are People . . . . . . . . . . 243

Chapter Twenty-Three: Spirit-Formed . . . . . . . . . . . . 261

Chapter Twenty-Four: Joy . . . . . . . . . . . . . . . . . . . . 275

Chapter Twenty-Five: Words . . . . . . . . . . . . . . . . . . 291

# INTRODUCTION

It was early, about 4:30 a.m., when He came and shut down my Bible study. Suddenly, unexpectedly, like a thick warm blanket, the Holy Spirit rested on me with a soft, startling, and purposeful presence.

"Sit up and write," He whispered. I grabbed a legal pad from the table and began to write everything I heard. "John; New Testament; baptism; marriage; communion..."

Like someone writing down directions being given too quickly, I scribbled what I heard.

Before this heavy presence lifted, I saw a picture of Jesus in my mind's eye. He was smiling and around His neck was a necklace made of very large pearls, each one unique.

I heard the Lord say, "Out of the ashes, I will bring forth a pearl. Many pearls will come forth and dwell close to My heart and bring honor to My name."

Out of this encounter, in 2011, the Higher Ground School of Ministry was born. We passionately embraced the sixty-seven classes the Lord downloaded to us. We soaked each topic in prayer and then shared what we were given over sixty-seven consecutive Wednesday evenings. We rejoiced with thirteen ministers who graduated from our first class. The school continues to bear good fruit through our online Higher Ground School of Ministry.

As of 2021, more than eighty "brothers-in-blue"

(prisoners) have graduated from our Satellite Campus in Putnam Prison.

We have watched this word come to pass.

We have witnessed many broken souls come to Christ and answer His call to ministry. Each precious soul is like the Pearl of Great Price found in the thirteenth chapter of Matthew's Gospel.

Along this journey, there have been other pearls also, pearls of discovery, pearls of truth.

In this book, *A Shepherd's Pearls*, I believe the Lord will highlight some of these pearls in such a way as to help and bless you in your calling. After all, we are all called! Some are called to business, some to music, some to raise a family, some to pulpit ministry, but we are all called. Why we do what we do is even more important than what we do.

One pearl of discovery is one I call the sweet spot of God's grace. When we go where the Lord says, "Go," and do what the Lord says, "Do," we will have joy and peace that is out of this world.

The story goes about two men laying bricks. A passerby asked one of the men, "What are you doing?"

He replied, "Can't you see; I'm laying bricks."

The inquisitive traveler asked the second bricklayer, "What are you doing?"

His reply was priceless, "Can't you see; I'm building a church."

So, let me ask you, are you just laying bricks, or are you building a church?

The sixty-seven-class curriculum of Higher Ground School of Ministry is now fully accredited. All of our precious ministry students memorize Ephesians 2:8–10,

> *For it is by grace you have been saved, through faith—and this is not from yourselves, it is the gift of God—not by works, so that no one can boast. For we are God's handiwork, created in Crist Jesus to do good works, which God prepared in advance for us to do.*

One of the pearls of truth each receives is "we don't work for grace. We work from grace, but we work!"

Some of our graduates now pastor churches in Kenya, Canada, and South Africa. Some have served as prison chaplains. Some serve as missionaries and evangelists. Some are homeless shelter coordinators, emergency room nurses, and more. All have touched our hearts and impacted many for Christ. All have embraced our simple battle cry of "information, impartation, and activation."

For more than twenty-five years now, Jean and I have been in full-time ministry, building His church. Along the way, we have encountered many precious people. In this book, I hope to introduce you to some of them and share some of the pearls of discovery we have made along the way.

God has blessed us in Billy Graham's board room and on death row. We have experienced His touch on the beautiful Sea of Galilee and in the slums and prisons of Honduras. God has graced us with wonderful "aha moments" teaching children's church and while graduating seminary; in the smoky AA rooms of the Bowery in New York and kayaking the cobalt blue ocean in Maui, Hawaii. God provided for us when we lived in one rented room with the bathroom outside in the hall, and He provides for us now as we manage a seven-figure estate and live on a 3-acre farm. God is faithful.

As I'm writing *A Shepherd's Pearls*, Jean and I just became great-grandparents! It boggles my mind to think my son is a grandpa. It's even more startling to think I am now sleeping with a great-grandmother!

As we celebrate God's grace in our golden years, we so want to leave a legacy of faith for our kids and grandkids and those we have been so humbly blessed to minister to.

I pray this book blesses you and encourages you to serve the Lord with all your heart for all your days. Scripture promises if we "seek Him with all our heart, we will find Him" (Jeremiah 29:13) (paraphrased by the author).

Whether you are a new believer or a seasoned saint, remember that there is always higher ground in God.

# CHAPTER ONE:

# HOW I MARVEL

*"If you want to change the world,*
*pick up your pen and write."*
**Martin Luther**

How I marvel at the handiwork of God. In the more than two score years I have walked with Jesus, I never cease to be amazed. His ways are different than our ways.

He is more faithful than the sunrise and yet so full of surprises. He is beyond definition. He is more unpredictable than the ocean, and yet His ebbs and flows have a rhythm sure enough.

His Word, the Holy Scriptures, is alive. My life, my wife and kids, our call, and every life are a sure evidence of this.

How quickly time flies. Hard to believe it will soon be half a century ago His strong Spirit and angels rescued a frustrated young father from the tyrannical clutches of alcoholism. That He did. He sent His Word to heal me on that morning, pained by the shame a hangover brings to a young Christian bound by the ruthless cycle of Romans 7, doing the thing one hates, not finding the power to carry out the call to please God with a sober walk.

"Even youths grow tired and weary, and young men stumble and fall; but those who hope in the Lord will renew their strength. They will soar on wings like eagles" (Isaiah 40:30–31).

Things of the Spirit remain eternally fresh. Though that liberating visitation occurred nearly a half-century ago, it is as if it happened yesterday.

This same strong Spirit that broke the shackles of chronic addiction off my life now compels me to write this book. But why? That I am not sure of. However, we walk by faith and slowly learn to yield to the prompting and leading of His Spirit (2 Corinthians 5:7; Romans 8:14).

Even now, as I include a couple of Scripture references, I find myself praying for you, who will, for some providential reason, read this. I pray that if these scriptures are not alive in you, you will pause and look them up, write them down, and hide them in your heart so that they may give you the same blessing, strength, and comfort as they have given me.

His Word is indeed alive! *Theopneutos*... "God-breathed." If we draw close enough to His Word, we can feel His very breath. The warmth of His whispers can and do melt the coldest, hardest hearts. His presence brings healing to the broken soul and the troubled mind. I know it is so. I am one such man.

Dr. Paul Hegstrom, founder of "Learning to Live, Learning to Love" and author of *Broken Children, Grown-Up Pain*, said: "If we are teachable, it is fixable." Ironic, isn't it? The older we get, the more fixable we can become.

Sure, there are exceptions to every rule. But consider Jesus' encounter with the woman caught in the act of adultery. Consider the response to His timeless command, "Let any one of you who is without sin be the first to throw a stone at her" (John 8:7). Wasn't it "the older ones" who dropped their stones first? Selah.

One of the liberating keys to the late Dr. Hegstrom's ministry is an emphasis on the simple truth we and we alone are responsible for our response to whatever we walk through.

I remember standing agog hearing Joyce Meyer speak of her childhood. As a kid, she was, for many years, raped by her biological father as her mother looked the other way. Joyce forgave them, bought them a house, led them to Christ, and before her father died, she baptized him!

Grace this big is bigger than me. Yet, I am humbled and strengthened to witness such grace is alive in some. It serves to remind me I have a long way to go in this quest to become like Jesus. Yes, "In this world we are like Jesus" (1 John 4:17), but, let's face it, some are more like Him than others!

What I really find flabbergasting about Joyce's testimony is she says, "I wouldn't change anything about my childhood because God used it to shape who I am." Wow! *Boom!* Drop the mic! Grace this big is surely bigger than me.

Such a godly response to such horror highlights the sovereignty of God. Did God want or intend for Joyce to be raped and repeatedly traumatized by her earthly father? No, of course not. But He worked good out of even that. He takes what the enemy intends for evil and, through His sovereign grace, works good out of it. Joyce didn't choose her parents; God did. However, Joyce and Joyce alone chose how she would respond to her trauma.

We are all works in progress. "When Christ appears, we shall be like him, for we shall see him as he is" (1 John 3:2). None of us have arrived. There is always higher ground in God. Where are you in your journey with Jesus? What is your next step forward in grace? Just asking.

"Everything can be taken from a man but one thing: the last of human freedoms—to choose one's attitude in any given set of circumstances."[1] This profundity was penned by Dr. Viktor Frankl. Frankl was a remarkable survivor of the horrors of Auschwitz, Dachau, and other treacherous Nazi death camps of WWII, where his family was dehumanized, tortured, and murdered.

I know what Dr. Frankl said is true, but to know a truth and walk out a truth are two very different things.

Abe Lincoln broke down the same truth in a way I can

more easily relate to. Honest Abe once said, "Most folks are as happy as they make up their minds to be."

Are you happy? Just asking.

With more than a quarter-century under my belt serving God's people (and some others) as a pastor, I wish I could say most Christians are happy, but I can't. I wish I could say most Christ-followers consistently walk uprightly in the truth, but I can't.

Perhaps that illuminates one of the heartbeats of this book. What if God could use the scribble of this senior citizen to help another sojourner? God is certainly able. Will He? You be the judge.

I have found the old cliché about working through difficulties to be true, "they will make you better or make you bitter." The choice is ours.

Henry Ford was right, "Whether you believe you can or believe you can't, either way you are right."

There is a lot of real estate between self-loathing and self-aggrandizement. Precisely in the middle of these two illusions is what I call "the sweet spot of God's grace." That is the place where John 5 and Philippians 4:13 converge. Let me explain.

In John 5:19, Jesus shares how "[he] can do nothing by himself." In Philippians 4:13, Paul says, "I can do all this through him who gives me strength." So there you have it! Apart from Him, we can do nothing (John 15:5), but through Him, we can do all things.

Personally, I believe only Jesus walked in this "sweet

spot of God's grace" from start to finish. The rest of us are "stumbling to glory." We spend most of our time either trying too hard to serve God in our own power or not being as engaged in His plan and purpose as we should be.

Perhaps I'm oversimplifying things, but there appear to be two groups of Christians in the church. One group needs help from the Holy Spirit to "get off their blessed assurance," get out of the pew and get their foot on the gas pedal. A second group seems to need help "putting their foot on the brakes" to stop their insane self-effort and religious busyness. Both groups need help from the Holy Spirit! Which group do you identify with? Just asking.

Along the way, we have those "aha moments" where we "know in our knower" we are right where the Lord wants us to be and doing precisely what He wants us to be doing.

A fellow pastor I served with on a *Kairos* prison weekend at Tomoka Prison used to say, "If you don't have joy serving Jesus, you're not doing it right." I agree with Pastor Z's statement. However, just a few days after the exhilarating closing ceremony of this amazing three-day mountaintop renewal weekend, Pastor Z committed suicide.

Evidently, Pastor Z "wasn't doing it right." He certainly wasn't practicing what he preached. He knew the truth but didn't walk it out. Why? Was it the weight of the world? Was it the pull or failings of the flesh? Was it the devil who always wants to steal, kill, and destroy (John 10:10)?

I believe it was all of the above.

Usually, when a Christian leader falls, it is one of the "three G's" that takes them out: "gold," "glory," or "girls" (or "guys" for lady leaders).

Those in full-time ministry seem to have a special target on their back. Some of my Vietnam Vet friends tell me that in combat situations, officers hide their stripes because their enemies are shrewd enough to understand taking out a leader hurts the entire platoon. So it is with the devil. He's crazy but not stupid.

Some recent survey results from the Barna Group concerning pastors are sobering:

- Ninety percent report ministry is completely different than what they thought.
- Ninety-five percent don't pray daily with their spouse.
- Seventy percent don't have a close friend.
- Fifty percent are overweight and don't exercise.
- Thirty-four percent visit porn sites.
- Ten percent retire as a pastor.

In our Higher Ground School of Ministry, one of the sixty-seven classes deals with the subject of "eternal security." It is not our goal to cajole students to any specific doctrinal position on the matter. Rather, our purpose in this class is to inform students about the history and beliefs of "Calvinists" vs. "Arminians," particularly regarding the "once saved, always saved, or not" argument.

One of the takeaways we hope ministry students will

glean from the class is how the very question of "once you're saved, can you lose your salvation?" is beyond a flawed question. It is really a stupid question.

Imagine if, when I fell in love with my beautiful wife, I knelt down and presented her with a ring and said, "Jean, I love you with all my heart and want to ask you to be my wife, but how far will you let me stray without filing for divorce?"

Do you see how crazy that is? That's why we believe that question can and should be replaced with a better question like:

- "Do you love Jesus?"

- "What was your life like B. C.?"

- "How did you come to Jesus?"

- "How has Jesus changed your life?"

- "When, most recently, has the Holy Spirit helped you?"

# Faith Challenge

Get a notebook, take a few minutes and answer the above questions. Write on the top of page one: Faith Challenge #1.

# CHAPTER TWO:

# THE BROKEN YEARS

*"It is during our darkest moments that we must focus to see the light."*

**Aristotle**

In his book, *Broken Children, Grown-Up Pain*, Dr. Paul Hegstrom does an excellent job explaining how we all see through our own "filters." We come from different backgrounds, and our perceptions and outlook are greatly impacted by our childhood and life experiences.

Some, like Joyce Meyers, grew up in a household with tremendous abuse. On the other extreme, many grow up with well-meaning parents that spoil and enable them.

Not everyone grew up with their father spoiling them. I sure didn't. My dad was the oldest of four kids, born in Ware Shoals, South Carolina, and grew up in neighboring Piedmont. His dad was a magistrate, and his mom worked in a cotton mill. They were poor. Even as an old man, Dad would make himself a big glass of cornbread and buttermilk. He said he enjoyed the taste. Perhaps he did. However, I believe it also served as a reminder of where he came from.

Dad was the first Eagle Scout in Piedmont. He worked his way through college at the University of South Carolina, joined the Army Air Corp during WWII, where he was a member of the U. S. Army Boxing Team, and earned the rank of captain. Dad's unequaled work ethic and his take-no-prisoners personality served him well. After just a few years of hard work as a manager of a local S. H. Kress store, senior management discovered him and recruited him to their home office on Madison Avenue in New York.

Summit, New Jersey, where I was born, was a bedroom community to New York City. Every morning Dad would take the Erie Lackawanna railroad to "The City" and then ride this beautiful train with its stylish wicker seats home. This was Dad's routine until I was about eight or nine years of age. Then he didn't come home every night. Then he came home less and less regularly. My sisters and I wouldn't dare ask where he had been. Did I mention Dad was a captain in the Army during WWII? Dad was always a captain. I was very much afraid of him when I was a child. Most people were.

But, before our home on beautiful Badeau Avenue in upscale Summit, New Jersey devolved into the longest and most bitter divorce I have ever witnessed, Dad gave each of us his work ethic.

As our neighborhood friends would ride their bicycles by our house on the weekends, we would be raking leaves or pulling weeds. I resented this at the time but have grown to realize that Dad was not being cruel. He was giving us a piece of himself.

My father-in-law, Joe (a loud 300-pound New York City firefighter), used to say, "You can't take a forty-year-old head and put it on twenty-year-old shoulders." Joe, God rest his soul, was so right. Our perspective changes with age.

As a kid, I didn't know if Dad was coming home less and less because Mom was drinking more and more or was Mom drinking more and more because Dad was coming home less and less.

Mom was nine years younger than Dad. They were married when Mom was seventeen. She no doubt idolized her Army Air Corp officer knight in shining armor, who swooped her off her feet and took the preacher's kid from a small southern town to see the world. My eldest sister, Tica, was born in San Juan, Puerto Rico, where Mom and Dad were stationed during the war.

*The Brisseys of Summit, N.J.*

No doubt Mom and Dad had some good years together. Mom was a talented artist who enjoyed her own art studio in our big three-story house in Summit. As a kid, I remember our dentist, Dr. Fotti, paid Mom fifty dollars for one of her paintings which he prominently hung in his waiting room. This was in the early 1960s. Fifty dollars was a lot of money back then.

Our home had many beautiful paintings Mom had painted. A leopard, a sailboat, paintings of ballerinas, birds, flowers, and much more. These works of art mysteriously disappeared during the last years of the bitter divorce.

My sister, Roxie, somehow saved the painting of the leopard that Mom painted in art school when she was eighteen. I always look forward to seeing it when I visit Roxie. I used to shoot it with my squirt gun when I was a kid. Somehow it survived. Somehow, so did we.

Peter tells us in 1 Peter 4:8, "Love covers over a multitude of sins." I experienced this truth long before I ever opened a Bible. Looking back, there was always one thing I knew as a kid, and that was that Mom loved me.

My first days in military school were shocking. That's where Dad sent me as our home slowly disintegrated. Roxie was sent to St. John's Episcopal boarding school just a few miles from General Douglas MacArthur Military Academy. As a twelve-year-old "plebe" (as they called us new cadets), I would lay on my bed and cry and pray. I could see the light on a tower a few miles away, and I knew that tower was near St. John's. I knew Roxie was there and was probably thinking of me as I was thinking of her. Somehow, that light softened the loneliness. Our sister, Tica, was going to high school and already winning beauty pageants while living with our grandparents in Piedmont.

Douglas MacArthur Military Academy, though a most unpleasant experience, may have saved my life. At the time, I detested sitting on the last two inches of my chair at a full brace and squaring my meals.

"Sir, yes, sir" and "Sir, no, sir" were our battle cries. The school was run by retired Army officers and attended by a colorful combination of West Point want-to-bes, disciplinary problem kids, and boys from divorced or divorcing homes.

The principal was Colonel Hoar. As you can imagine, we cadets had fun with his name. Colonel Hoar took special delight in writing demerits as a result of the most minor infraction during our weekly Saturday morning white glove inspections. Each demerit was worked off by one hour of marching with an M-1 rifle after school. There was never a shortage of cadets marching around the compound for a few hours after school each day. I can still hear the cadence being called out as they (or we) marched. Calling cadence became an art form reserved for only the best-drilled cadets.

I disliked military school, but it was good for me. After supper each night, all cadets were required to sit silently at their fold-out chair-desk with their book bags at their side for two hours. That was the rule. In military school, you learn to follow the rules. No one was required to even open a book. However, out of sheer boredom, I began to open my textbooks.

During those mandatory study times, I made two discoveries. One discovery was that I was not stupid. Up until that season in my life, I was convinced I was stupid. Failing the third grade can do that to a guy. Secondly, I discovered that when I read the homework assignments, I could answer questions the next day in class. I liked that a lot.

Soon I began to enjoy studying. For the first time in my life, I was making the honor roll, and that seemed to make Dad proud. His letters became more frequent and more positive. I worked hard to make Dad proud. Soon I was promoted to private first class, then corporal, then the first seventh-grade cadet to earn the rank of sergeant. I received a special letter of congratulations in the mail when I won the Best Drilled Cadet award.

Dad was proud of his Cadet Sergeant Brissey. So much so that on one of his monthly visits, he got special permission to take me to see the New York Giants play football. As much as I loved the Giants, I was disappointed Dad made me wear my dress blue uniform to the game. I felt like a freak, but I would never tell Dad that. "Sir, yes, sir" was the order of the day.

Looking back, I can see Dad tried. In his own way, he really tried. He once took me to the World Series to see the Yankees play the Cardinals. Seeing my hero, Mickey Mantle, play in a World Series would have been phenomenal if I wasn't so afraid of Dad. He was a big authoritative guy, and being in his presence was intimidating.

Mom sure tried also. She stayed in Summit as long as she could so she could be near Roxie and me, even though we were in boarding schools. I was permitted to go home from General Douglas MacArthur Military School one weekend a month.

On one such weekend in February of 1968, I went home to Badeau Avenue in Summit, New Jersey, to find Mom alone in the house with no heat or electricity. I have a picture etched in my mind of walking into the kitchen and finding Mom in her full-length fur coat staring out the window in a semi-catatonic state.

Many years later, as I was going through theophostic counseling, I asked the Lord, "Where were You, Lord, on that day that I walked into that cold, lonely house to find my mom staring out the window?"

He showed me a picture of Him standing with her, holding her up with both His arms wrapped around her. Jesus was with her. He is faithful. He never left Mom. He never leaves us. Even when we don't recognize Him, He sustains us.

Mom soon moved back to North Carolina to live with her mom. Our grandmother, "Mornin'," as she was called, was an amazing and loving Christian woman. She was the organist in my grandfather, Rev. Fred Lineberger's church. Like Mom, she was also seventeen when she married. For several years after my grandfather had a debilitating stroke, Mornin' bathed and dressed the love of her life every day until his death.

Mom lived with Mornin' on Lillian Rd. In Wilson, North Carolina, Mornin' taught more than a hundred piano students per week. Mom and Dad's divorce proceedings slowly ground forward. One of the reasons my parent's divorce took so long was Mom, in spite of her emotional instabilities, was doggedly determined not to agree with my dad's demand that she legally change her surname back to her maiden name of Lineberger.

I was fifteen years old when my parent's divorce was finalized. I was then attending Coindre Hall, a Catholic boarding school on Long Island, even though I had never been to a Catholic church.

Very soon after my parent's divorce, I volunteered to be the best man at my dad's wedding. As Dad exchanged marriage vows with "Mrs. S," I felt like the worst man, not the best man. But, alas, the mystery was solved as to where dad was all of those nights he didn't come home.

At the ripe old age of seventeen, I left my dad and his strict oversight to live with my mom and Roxie. Mom was healthy enough to move to New York and, in so doing, empowered me to attend the City University of New York at Brooklyn College. I gave the pre-med program at Brooklyn College the old college try for three years but was way out of my league scholastically.

I took a five-credit anatomy course in the summer of 1976. That's when Jean and I met, fell in love, got pregnant, and got married. Did I mention I was studying anatomy that summer?

I had a blue Kawasaki. Jean had a yellow bikini. I dropped out of college and went to work, first selling life insurance, then selling radio advertising, then as a waiter in New York City. We knew our marriage was made in heaven because of all the thunder and lightning!

After having a "road to Damascus" conversion

experience on January 21, 1979, I never questioned the authenticity or inerrancy of the Bible...except for one passage of Scripture. Romans 8:28 says, "And we know that in all things God works for the good of those who love him, who have been called according to his purpose."

You see, the day I memorized that verse, I was in what I refer to as my "Romans 7 season." The good I wanted to do (live for God and honor my family) I couldn't find the power to do. That which I didn't want to do (get drunk and disgrace my Lord and my family) I kept doing.

I attended AA meetings every day. Some days I made two meetings. I memorized Scripture and prayed all the time. After about thirty days, a fellow waiter would suggest we get a cold beer after work. My insanity was, despite failing countless times to "drink just one beer," I would actually believe "this time will be different...I will drink one beer and go home."

One beer would lead to two, then three, then at some point, I would lose count. So it was on the day I memorized Romans 8:28. Waking up on the F-train in Queens, New York, during rush hour the morning after "going to get one beer" was as terrifying as it was humiliating.

I staggered off that subway, shaking my fist at heaven. "So, You say You work *all things* together for my good? How in heaven's name will You work good out of this?"

In time, He has done just that! As years went by and "one day at a time" resulted in one year's sobriety...then five...then ten...now four decades, I would sometimes be tempted to pat myself on the back. "Good sermon, Pastor." "Did a hundred men come forward to the altar during Christmas Eve service at Putnam Prison, Pastor?" "I enjoyed your book, Pastor."

Countless times, before patting myself on the back, the Lord would bring me back to that F-train. "If it were not for My grace, son, that's where you would be."

Scripture tells us in 2 Corinthians 12:7 that the apostle Paul was "given a thorn in the flesh to keep him humble" (paraphrased by the author).

Yes, God's Word is true. All of it. Even Romans 8:28. A popular bumper sticker once said, "God said it. I believe it. That settles it." Personally, I believe it would be more accurate to say, "God said it. That settles it."

His Word is settled in heaven. If we, by God's grace, believe it, we are blessed. Those who choose to deny the truth of Scripture shortchange themselves, but His Word remains settled for all time.

Let me ask you:

- How has God brought good out of hardship or suffering in your life?

- Have you ever experienced a "Romans 7" season in your life? When and where?

- When was the last time you memorized a Scripture verse? What does it say?

- How has your perspective changed over the last twenty years?

# Faith Challenge

Take a few minutes and write the above questions and
your answers in your notebook.

# A Pearl of Sacrifice

There must be a purpose to all of this, I thought as I walked into Howard Hall. It was welcoming day at military school. The first soldier I met greeted me with a sinister grin and circled my head with a shaver. I was in shock from losing all my hair so abruptly. The wool from the West Point uniform was scratchy and uncomfortable, and the hat they issued me was way too tight on my head. Dad sent me here…so it must be for a purpose.

The weeks and months that followed were filled with formations, marching drills, and white-glove inspections. We squared our meals and our shoulders. We cleaned our plates, our rifles, and our rooms and shouted "Sir, yes, sir" at the top of our lungs. The cadets of B Company shared many hard-earned lessons. We learned discipline, duty, and honor, and to salute when the stars and stripes were raised. Never had I felt so alone… never had I been so very far from home.

It was just before the commencement exercises when I got my sergeant's stripes. My dad was so proud. He had been a captain in World War II. I think my father loved me most on the day I got my stripes.

As I reminisce about my time at General Douglas MacArthur Military Academy, I'm reminded of my father's favorite verse: "For God so loved the world that he gave his one and only Son" (John 3:16). I wonder if Jesus was in shock when He lost His beard so abruptly or if the soldiers met Him with a sinister grin. How hard it must have been for Him to wear His purple robe... how sharp His crown of thorns must have been, so tightly fitted on His head.

"For the joy set before him he endured the cross" (Hebrews 12:2b), the writer of Hebrews says. Yet nothing is said of how lonely He must have felt, so very far from home. Could it be the Father loved Him most on the day He got His stripes?

Oh, Christian, think it not a small thing, this duty He saw through. The whip, the cross, and the empty tomb were given for you and me. He loves us in the valley...He loves us on mountain heights.

I think the Father loves us most on days we get our stripes!

# CHAPTER THREE:

# PRESSING ON

*"Try not to become a person of success, but rather try to become a person of value."*

**Albert Einstein**

As we press on together in this chapter, I do pray you will stay engaged. I have felt impressed to share some personal testimony in hopes you will understand the frame of reference from which I wish to share some of the pearls of truth God has revealed since that fateful day many years ago when we took the leap of faith into full-time ministry.

As I often say, "A person with a testimony is never at the mercy of a man with an argument." My ambition is not to argue theology. Rather, my hope is to inspire and challenge you in the truth.

Story goes about a six-year-old little girl who was busy

drawing a picture with crayons on her construction paper during her first-grade class. The teacher walked by and inquired, "What are you drawing, Sally?"

The diligent young artist answered, "I'm drawing a picture of God."

The teacher answered by saying, "But, Sally, no one knows what God looks like."

Sally didn't miss a beat. "They will in a minute!"

We all have a slightly different picture of God in our mind's eye. My hope is not to sell you my picture. However, if the Holy Spirit will grace this scribble, I believe together we can add some color to your picture of who He is in your life.

God is no respecter of persons. Jesus is the same yesterday, today, and forever. Yet, our perceptions may vary tremendously. In his book, *Broken Children, Grown-Up Pain*, Dr. Paul Hegstrom shares how we all see through our own filters, which have been shaped by our own life experiences.

Hegstrom goes on to explain how we can become "arrested in development." He explains, scientifically, how our brains physiologically handle trauma. Thank God Paul Hegstrom also sheds light on how we can, through specific prayer for a specific need, receive breakthroughs over the traumas of our past. It's fascinating, really, how fearfully and wonderfully made we are!

*The greatest power within a person is the ability to choose change. This requires self-examination, this requires determination, this requires judging what needs to be changed, this requires moving from shame into guilt, and this requires repentance.*

Man's Search for Meaning
**Viktor Frankl**

This powerful truth goes hand in glove with Victor Frankl's discovery regarding our irrefutable God-given ability to "choose how we will respond" to various trauma or stimuli. It also lines up with Jesus' promise of John 8:32, "Then you will know the truth, and the truth will set you free."

There is an unmistakable relationship between truth, freedom, and repentance. The truth is we need the help of the Spirit of truth, the blessed Holy Spirit, to even know the truth.

In AA, we say, "You're only as sick as your secrets." When we surrender the facade and get "rigorously honest" with ourselves, we begin to understand what Jeremiah was pointing to in Jeremiah 17:9 when he said, "The heart is deceitful above all things and beyond cure. Who can understand it?"

I used to think the deceitfulness of our hearts was our propensity to "wear masks" and not be transparent or authentic with others. I have come to discover that the real deceitfulness of our hearts is in its cunning ability to deceive ourselves!

"If we claim to be without sin, we deceive ourselves and the truth is not in us. If we confess our sin, he is faithful and just and will forgive us our sins and purify us from all sin" (1 John 1:8–9).

John 6:44, Jesus tells us, "No one can come to me unless the Father who sent me draws them." Without His help, we can't even come to Him. How could we think we could grow up in Him on our own without His help?

God has His ways of helping us "press on" to higher ground, and there is always higher ground in God. This "confession and repentance" thing is not a one-shot deal. It is a lifestyle and a blueprint for growing in the grace and knowledge of who Jesus is. Humility is key.

Andrew Murray once said, "Humility is not so much a grace or virtue along with others; it is the root of all, because it alone takes the right attitude before God, and allows Him as God to do all."

When we were in Bethlehem, we were so blessed to visit the famous Church of the Nativity, located at the spot where historians believe Jesus was born. It was surreal. However, to enter this holy sight, one must bow down to enter a small doorway known as "the gate of humility." And so it is with our God.

It was a defining moment for me more than forty years ago at an AA meeting in Astoria, Queens, to speak the words for the first time, "Hello, my name is Jim, and I'm an alcoholic."

The Bible is so right. God gives grace to the humble

but opposes the proud. The truth is it wasn't Bill W., one of the founders of AA, who taught us we should live one day at a time. It was Jesus in Matthew chapter 6. Each day has its own challenges, but the same God who is watching over the sparrows is watching over us!

Each of us is a unique unduplicatable miracle of God. Each of us has our own unique strengths and weaknesses. Each of us has our own unique areas where we can be tempted.

My good friend, James "Gator" Leggett, says, "The devil knows where our goat is tied up." Gator knows what he's talking about. He spent almost nineteen years in prison for shooting his ex-wife six times in the head and killing her.

His victim's brother heard his sister had been murdered, grabbed his shotgun, and was on his way to take Gator off the planet. The sheriff got there first. James would certainly have gotten the death penalty, but his victim's parents were Christian ministers who opposed the death penalty. Gator received a forty-year sentence and served almost nineteen years behind bars.

Gator's former brother-in-law, Burt, swore he was going to kill Gator whenever he was released from prison. Burt even used Gator's expected release date as his PIN number. Every single time Burt would use his debit card, he would tell himself, "This is the date I will avenge Vera's death."

Well, as someone once said, "If you want to make God laugh, tell Him *your* plans." Once Gator was finally released from prison, he and Burt had an unexpected reunion during a *Kairos* prison ministry meeting. Instead of killing Gator, Burt was overcome with emotions, and the two men hugged and cried.

Now they minister together on *Kairos* prison ministry weekends. On day one, Gator shares how he needed God's grace to forgive himself for taking a precious life. On day two, Burt gets up and shares how he needed God's help to forgive the man who murdered his precious sister. On day three, both Gator and Burt stand up, and Burt points to Gator and says, "This is the man who killed my sister." *Boom!* Drop the mic!

The good news is God is not finished with any of us. He who has begun a good work in us will bring it on to completion (Philippians 1:6).

Perhaps you don't struggle with alcoholism or substance abuse. Perhaps you have never been arrested or spent any time in jail. Perhaps no one has murdered one of your loved ones. The truth is "we all have fallen short" of God's standard of holiness. We all, like sheep, have gone astray in our own way. If we are honest, we all have something in common. We all need to repent. The Greek word is *metanoia*. It means to "have a change of mind and to change directions."

As we journey through life, there are people we need to forgive. Perhaps it's our mom or dad, a sibling, a spouse, an employer, a pastor, or maybe it's ourselves.

A few years after I was born again, I was earnestly

trying to "live the golden rule" and to "love others as I loved myself." One day, as I was in prayer, the Holy Spirit visited me. God used a picture in my mind's eye to show me what my problem was in "loving my neighbor as myself." He showed me I didn't love myself.

The vivid picture He showed me is just as clear in my mind right now as it was some thirty-eight years ago. I saw a picture of Jesus being crucified. He was still alive in agony on the cross. I saw a man standing in front of the cross. He was spitting on the cross. As the picture unfolded over the man's shoulder, I saw that man was me!

I said, "Lord...I would never spit on Your cross."

The Lord said, "Every time you don't forgive yourself, *that* is exactly what you are doing." I repented that day for not forgiving myself.

## Faith Challenge Questions

Write these questions down in your notebook. Pray about them. Write out your responses:

- If you drew a picture of God, what would He look like? Is He happy, sad, or angry?

- Do you recognize any areas in your life in which God would have you change?

- In what area does the devil tempt you?

- On a scale of 1 to 10 (with 10 being the highest), how humble are you?

- Who do you need to forgive?

# CHAPTER FOUR:

# COME, HOLY SPIRIT

*"In my country, we go to prison first
and then become president."*

**Nelson Mandela**

When Jean, our two precious young children, and I moved from New York to Tampa, Florida, in 1985, we joined Holy Trinity Lutheran Church. That's where my mom and uncles and cousins worshipped. The first Sunday we attended, my cousin Rick was being ordained and installed as a Lutheran pastor.

Although we did our utmost to serve the Lord there, we felt as out of place as a milk bucket under a bull. We were zealous in our faith but were so young, immature, and untrained. We knew nothing about being "rightly fitted" with like-minded believers.

The short liturgical services left us feeling like there

should be more. There was one other "Charismatic" believer in the church. The three of us were the only ones who lifted our hands to heaven during worship. We felt like oddballs.

*"The Original Four"*

There were many precious folks at Holy Trinity. While we attended Holy Trinity, Jean was invited to serve as president of the women's gild. She accepted. She started her first meeting by reading from the Scriptures. She closed her first meeting as their leader by asking the women to be sure to bring their Bibles to the next meeting.

One elderly woman tried to coach Jean on "how they did things there." "We don't bring our Bibles...we just want to have tea." That outspoken naysayer suddenly and unexpectedly died shortly after that! Coincidence? Probably, but the ladies started bringing their Bibles.

I was appointed to head up their evangelism ministry. I had no idea what I was doing other than sharing how Jesus changed my life. These many years later, I see, in my *naïveté*, that I was on target.

During our season at Holy Trinity, the door opened for us to serve on *Via de Cristo* Christian renewal weekends. Serving on these grace-filled three-day weekends revolutionized our walk with Christ.

The format for the *Via de Cristo* was first discovered by a Catholic priest in Majorca, Spain, in the 1950s. He called it *"Cursillo,"* which just means "a short course."

This "short course in Christianity" spread all over the world and, depending on denominational affiliation, goes by different names: *Cursillo, Via de Cristo, Walk to Emmaus, Tres Días*, and *Kairos* (prison). The lifeblood of each is prayer and servanthood.

The "pre-prayeration" for each weekend takes place during ten weekly team meetings. Men meet with men in preparation for "the men's weekend," followed by the women's team meetings and women's weekend. Each team consists of about fifty to sixty believers from a few dozen different churches from a dozen or so denominations. This living tapestry of faith is as vibrant as it is diverse.

Augustine is credited for saying, "Unity in the essentials. Diversity in the non-essentials. Charity in all things." I know of no better demonstration of these ideals than the celebration which takes place as Catholics, Baptists, Presbyterians, and Episcopalians sit at the table with Lutherans, Methodists, and Pentecostals and those who claim allegiance to interdenominational expressions.

Jesus spoke truth when He said, "And I, when I am lifted up from the earth, will draw all people to myself" (John 12:32). As Jesus is lifted high and "the main thing remains the main thing," hearts catch fire with the same heartwarming experienced by the two disciples who walked with our resurrected Brother-King on the Road to Emmaus. "Were not our hearts burning within us while he talked with us on the road and opened the Scripture to us?" (Luke 24:32).

So, what is this "main thing" of which I speak? I'm so glad you asked! After all these years of walking with Jesus, I can tell you with full assurance that the most important thing in life, regardless of denominational pedigree or background, is to walk closely in a first love relationship with Jesus.

Are you walking closely with Jesus now? Do you sense the warmth of His presence?

If your answer is "yes," you are blessed. If your honest answer is "no," you are still blessed. You are still blessed because you *can* draw close right now. On *Via de Cristo* and *Kairos*, we pray a wonderful prayer. I invite you to pray right now:

"Come, Holy Spirit, fill the hearts of Your faithful and kindle in us the fire of Your Spirit. Send forth Your Spirit, and we shall be created, and You shall renew the face of the earth."

Why am I so sure this prayer is effective? By God's grace, in serving on more than fifty *Via de Cristo* weekends, I have watched with my own eyes the beautiful transformation that takes place when sinful souls collide with the unfathomable love and grace of God. I have witnessed too many to share.

On a *Kairos* prison weekend in November of 1995, I had a front-row seat as Inmate Thomas Duckett surrendered his life to Christ. Tom was three years into serving his five consecutive life sentences. While driving drunk, Tom was responsible for a horrific accident in which five precious lives were lost, and many more were forever impacted.

When I first met Tom, I thought he had a back deformity; he was so hunched over. During our table's chapel visit, as Tom called upon the Lord, he supernaturally straightened up right before my eyes. It was "the real deal." Inmate Duckett became a new creation in Christ and "a Timothy" to us at the same time.

Over the next twenty-five years of his incarceration, Tom "paid it forward" in many ways, including serving other "brothers-in-blue" on thirty-six subsequent *Kairos* weekends at different prisons. He also served as a main chaplain's assistant to three or four chaplains in different prisons.

Several years ago, God led us to bring our Higher Ground School of Ministry to Putnam Prison, where we had held outreaches for the past twenty years. By God's design, Tom was transferred to Putnam C. I. at the exact time we needed him there. He went through HGSM, was licensed, and served as our administrator for the next six cycles of sixty-seven classes. Tom helped more than fifty inmates graduate Higher Ground School of Ministry at Putnam Prison.

Tom's five life sentences were reduced, and he was released from prison after twenty-seven years, 111 days, on January 1, 2020. Being there to welcome him back to the free world was a great joy. After a bountiful breakfast at Cracker Barrel followed by Mahi Tacos on the Sunglow Pier in Daytona Beach, we drove home to our house, where Jean had a delicious pot roast dinner waiting. We were mega-blessed to have Tom spend his first night as a free man as our guest of honor.

On January 2, Tom checked into The GAP House, a local transition house for ex-prisoners. He wasted no time in serving at our church in any way he could. He took a job washing dishes and then landed a job in customer service at a communication company.

Right around the time God opened the door for Tom to move into his own duplex (a half-mile from our church) with his own one-year lease, the Lord moved on the heart of the leaders at The Bridge (a brand new state-of-the-art low barrier mission with thirty-four beds) to hire Tom full time where he now serves as shelter coordinator.

God can make a way where there is no way. He is a way-making, life-changing, attitude-rearranging, fear & bondage-busting God, and He loves us with an everlasting love!

*Tom Duckett - first night home after 27 yrs. in prison*

Tom now serves as a deacon in our church as an online instructor in Higher Ground School of Ministry and leads a monthly discipleship class at The Bridge. More importantly, Tom walks into a close personal first love relationship with Jesus and shares his testimony at the drop of a hat.

Yes! The main thing is to keep the main thing the main thing, and the main thing is walking in a close first love relationship with Jesus.

# Faith Challenge Questions

- On a scale from 1 to 10, with 1 being ice cold and 10 being red hot, how on-fire is your relationship with Jesus?

- Have you had trouble or disappointment trying to serve in church?

- Have past failures or disappointments hindered your walk with Jesus? If so, when and how?

# A Pearl of Promise

## God's Rainbow

*"I have set my rainbow in the clouds"*
**(Genesis 9:13).**

*Many colors make the rainbow,*
*All shining in one accord;*
*United by His promise*
*Is the rainbow of the Lord.*

*They say it takes not only rain*
*But also bright sunshine*
*Before we all can clearly see*
*His ribbon so divine.*

*Without all its bright colors,*
*The rainbow's incomplete.*
*Before He went to Calvary,*
*He washed His good friends' feet.*

*He took our sin at Calvary,*
*We know He despised the shame:*

*But for full joy endured the cross*
*And said, "I'll rise Again!"*

*Like Joseph's coat of colors*
*Once new, but then was torn*
*So did the Son of Man become,*
*As He wore His crown of thorns.*

*The promise of the Father,*
*The Son gave all He could,*
*Angels standing ready*
*As the spikes went into the wood.*

*"Father, please forgive them,*
*For they know not what they do!"*
*If I may be so bold, my friend:*
*Has He forgiven you?*

*Oh, blessed be the rainbow,*
*The rainbow of the king;*
*Colored with joy and victory,*
*He died to steal death's sting!*

*He rose again as He said He would,*
*I'm sure you know the story;*
*But do you know the mystery*

*Of Christ in you, the hope of glory?*

*There's forgiveness in no other,*
*The price He paid was great,*
*So seek the man from Galilee*
*Before it is too late.*

*To err is human, said the poet,*
*Forgiveness is divine.*
*He'll turn your sorrow into joy,*
*So receive the Son and shine.*

*Oh, blessed be God's rainbow,*
*Made of all those born again.*
*Oh, blessed be God's rainbow,*
*His rainbow's made of men!*

# CHAPTER FIVE:

# Kairos—God's Special Time

*"Tell me and I forget. Teach me and I remember.*
*Involve me and I learn."*

**Ben Franklin**

The rabbis of old focused much of their study on three areas: the Scriptures, nature, and people. We see the fruit of this focus throughout Scripture. So much of what Jesus preached referenced Old Testament scriptures. This is a great help when we realize the best way to interpret Scripture is with Scripture, line upon line, and precept upon precept.

The study of nature and people is also key to understanding our spiritual growth and development. Consider Hebrews chapter 11. We refer to this chapter of the Bible as "the faith chapter." Upon close examination, we see the author, time and again, point to how God mixes with men and women. The result is blessing, breakthrough, and transformation.

As you continue reading this book, it is my prayer the Holy Spirit will illuminate truths that will build and challenge your faith walk. When I mention a certain someone, I do hope you will recognize the method of my madness and allow the Lord to speak to your heart.

My purpose is not to simply convey some biological or historical information but to use their life or experience as a lens through which we can see the handiwork of God.

The words "cookies" and "color-books" may not prompt any special memories in you. To me, these two words, often associated with child's play, provoke a flood of God-incidences.

During our *Kairos* prison weekends, scores of loving, prayerful souls make more than a thousand delicious home-baked cookies just before the weekend begins, so they are fresh. As the weekend unfolds, a bottomless assortment of home-baked cookies is placed in the center of each of several round tables.

Each table is surrounded by three or four free men with three or four prisoners. As various talks and testimonies take place, brothers-in-blue feast on the unusually tasty baked treats. This one feature of the *Kairos* weekends is so enjoyed word spreads quickly throughout the prison compound. So much so that many of the inmates sign up for *Kairos* just "for the cookies."

In Romans 2:4, Paul points to the spiritual dynamite lurking behind the endless trays of home-baked cookies. He says, "Don't you know it is the kindness of God which leads to repentance" (paraphrased by the author).

As the three-day *Kairos* unfolds, the spirit of love behind the home-baked cookies is combined with hundreds of prayers that soak every cookie, every testimony, every song, and every prisoner. Prayer combined with purposeful actions achieve their divine purpose. God's goodness and kindness soften even the hardest of hearts to receive the good news of Jesus and His love.

Another surprising and unusual vehicle of grace the Lord uses on these *Kairos* weekends is in the form of children's crayoned drawings. Children draw pictures and sign their first name and age to the bottom of the drawing. The innocence of the children expressed with these funny drawings and misspelled words shine like diamonds in the dark prison culture.

We review these colorful portraits of grace before they are distributed to our new prisoner friends. As we were going through the children's drawings before one *Kairos* weekend, we came across a skillful depiction of an inmate in a striped uniform standing behind bars.

The seven-year-old artist had written a caption underneath his drawing in bold black crayon the words, "Bad. Bad. Bad." After enjoying a good laugh, we removed the drawing from the pile.

Without intending to, this little boy was giving voice

to what many people believe about the million-plus men and women incarcerated in our nation. The truth is these men and women are not imprisoned because of the crime they committed. They are incarcerated because they got caught.

There are many lawbreakers walking our streets and living in our neighborhoods who simply have not been caught. Having served in more than a dozen prisons in the U. S. and a couple in Honduras over the past twenty-five years, I can tell you most of the men and women in jail or prison are not any different from you or me.

Most did something stupid while under the influence of drugs or alcohol. That doesn't make it right. However, it does help illustrate the difference between guilt and shame. Guilt says, "You did something bad." Shame says, "You are bad." We are all guilty of breaking God's law, but because of Jesus, we no longer have to be ashamed.

Brennan Manning says it well in his book, *The Ragamuffin Gospel*: "The language of unhealthy guilt is harsh. It is demanding, abusing, criticizing, rejecting, blaming, condemning, reproaching and scolding."

On one *Kairos* weekend, the inmate sitting to my right (I will call him Sam) appeared to have a wall up the entire weekend. Nothing seemed to penetrate the ironclad defenses Sam had up to protect him in the prison hate factory he called home. All weekend, I wondered if he was getting anything at all out of the weekend.

On the last day of the weekend, when the children's

drawings were handed out, Sam broke down in tears. This silent shell of a man suddenly stood up and, in a loud voice, commanded everyone to be quiet and listen to what he had to say. He then held up his drawing, a simple color-book page signed by "Andrea, age nine."

Sam explained that he had a daughter named Andrea, who died during Hurricane Andrew in South Florida because he wasn't there to protect her. His daughter Andrea was nine when she died. All the walls around Sam crashed to the ground, not because of a Joshua shout, but because of a nine-year-old little girl's drawing. In his broken and humbled condition, Sam invited Jesus into his heart and was gloriously saved.

The point of the "cookies and the color-books" is as powerful as it is simple. Paul was right. The kindness of God, especially when soaked in prayer, leads even the hardest heart to repentance.

Gary Wilkerson puts it this way in his book, *David Wilkerson*. Gary says, "You have to be convinced, no matter what you are going through, you are loved."

There are other powerful testimonies of prisoners I hope to share later. Such as my friend Manny Valle, who was executed at Florida State Prison after thirty-three years on death row for killing a cop.

However, the heartbeat of this book is not to chronicle prisoners, people, or events. It is my prayer the light of God's Spirit will illuminate truth. I pray these truths will help you grow and go in God and, perhaps, avoid some of the same mistakes I have made in my almost seven decades.

Mother Theresa once said,

> *The greatest disease ...is not TB or leprosy; it is being unwanted, unloved, and uncared for. We can cure physical diseases with medicine, but the only cure for loneliness, despair, and hopelessness is love.*

> *A Simple Path*
> **Mother Teresa**

In *Kairos*, we speak of the "four L's." These four L's are not confined to the prison environment. They are effective tools anywhere, "listen, listen, love, love."

Paul was right. Love never fails.

# Faith Challenge Questions

When has your heart been touched
by the kindness of another's unselfish actions?

When was the last time you expressed
kindness to a stranger?

Have you ever been bound by shame?
If so, how did you overcome your shame?

Have you ever felt lonely or unloved?
Do you feel lonely or unloved right now?

On a scale of 1 to 10, how good of a listener are you?
How can you improve?

# CHAPTER SIX:

# TEN THOUSAND COUNSELORS

*"If there is no struggle, there is no progress."*

**Frederick Douglass**

First Corinthians 4:15 says, "Even if you had ten thousand guardians [instructors] in Christ, you do not have many fathers."

I have heard many a sermon with this scripture as a reference. Invariably, the content of such messages always seems to lean into the importance of spiritual fathers, mentors, etc. I've yet to hear anyone focus on what Paul says about the "ten thousand instructors." Some translations say, "ten thousand counselors."

How could we possibly have 10,000 instructors? If we do the math, that would be a new instructor every day for more than twenty-five years! What could this mean?

As I mentioned, the rabbis of old embraced three main streams of study in their relationship with God: God's Word, nature, and people. Could it be these 10,000 instructors could include the birds of the air and people we encounter as well as the Scriptures?

One thing is for certain, we can learn from each other. Someone once said, "When the student is ready, the teacher will appear." If we are listening and if we are teachable, we will certainly learn many new things and grow in our wisdom and understanding. As I mentioned, Dr. Paul Hegstrom spoke a powerful truth when he said, "If we are teachable, it is fixable."

One of the "instructors" God graced my life with was my father-in-law, Joe. Joe was a big, loud 300-pound New York City fireman. After fighting fires in Queens, New York, for twenty-two years, Joe enjoyed some good years with his wife. He then fought the raging blaze of cancer for seven years before he died.

I promise you, if you ever met him even once, you would never forget him. He was what we New Yorkers lovingly refer to as "a piece of work" or "a character." Joe did not have extensive formal education, but he had a double portion of street smarts.

As I mentioned earlier, one of Joe's many sayings was, "You can't take a forty-year-old head and stick it on twenty-year-old shoulders."

Let me illustrate Joe's point. Regardless of how old you are right now, can you remember how you looked at life fifteen to twenty years ago? Our perspective changes as we grow older. Whether we call it metamorphosis or the cycle of life, as was popularized in the movie, *The Lion King*, we must agree the aging process changes our perspective.

It is my heartfelt prayer that some of what I have learned and discovered in my journey will help you who read this book. You see, most of the pearls referred to in *A Shepherd's Pearls* do not originate with me. They have been gathered along the journey and adopted as my own.

Once you receive an illumination or an "aha moment" from a given truth or insight, it is then yours. As I mentioned, in our Higher Ground School of Ministry, we speak of "information, impartation, and activation."

For example, some years ago, my wife, Jean, led an outreach team and held an evangelistic service at Putnam Prison in East Palatka, Florida. After leading an anointed service with testimonies and a gospel message, Jean was impressed by the Lord to call on one of our deacons, Kevin, to give the invitation for those in the chapel to come to Christ. Kevin did a fine job, and several brothers-in-blue came forward and received Christ.

A few days after the service, Kevin came to me and said, "Pastor Jim, I hope it's okay, but when Pastor Jean called on me to give the altar call, I said everything you always say."

Despite Kevin's almost apologetic tone, I had to smile. You see, Kevin had been in so many meetings and listened to me give so many altar calls that he had internalized (imparted) the same scriptures God had equipped me with.

Many years ago, as I began "throwing out the net" and inviting people to receive Christ, the Holy Spirit prompted me to boldly proclaim.

First John 1:8–9, "If we claim to be without sin, we deceive ourselves and the truth is not in us. If we confess our sin, he is faithful and just and will forgive us our sins and purify us from all unrighteousness."

I assured Kevin he had done nothing wrong! Quite the contrary, with a teachable spirit, Kevin had adopted and internalized the same powerful pearls of truth John the Beloved shares in his first letter.

These illuminations and impartations can come from a variety of "instructors": books, birds, Scripture, or the quiet whispers of the Spirit.

A few years ago, Jean and I were mega-blessed with a large inheritance which included a 3-acre aspidistra farm in a bird sanctuary. That old hymn, "In the Garden," has taken on new life and meaning ever since.

*I come to the garden alone,*
*While the dew is still on the roses,*
*And the voice I hear falling on my ear,*
*The Son of God discloses.*
*And He walks with me, and He talks with me,*
*And He tells me I am His own*
*And the joy we share as we tarry there,*
*None other has ever known.*

This old classic so aptly describes the last few years

of my life. I have so enjoyed the sweet presence of Jesus while tilling the soil to grow tomatoes, broccoli, oranges, flowers, and more.

One quiet morning, as I was listening to the birds sing their morning songs, I heard the Lord whisper, "That is the original praise."

Immediately my mind was quickened to Psalm 150:6, where the psalmist says, "Let everything that has breath praise the Lord."

I was reminded how, in Genesis, the birds were created before us humans. Wow! This symphony being offered by our feathery friends was, indeed, "the original praise."

Later that morning, as I was enjoying quite a workout tilling the soil and planting and caring for my vegetables, the Holy Spirit whispered, "This is the original worship."

Immediately my mind was quickened to recall Romans 12 and Paul's admonition for us to "offer our bodies as living sacrifices." Scripture tells us this is our reasonable act of worship.

Again, I was reminded of the book of Genesis and how God's first charge to Adam was to take care of the Garden of Eden. This sweet presence of the Lord I was experiencing as I was working in the garden was, indeed, "the original worship."

Whether we receive instruction from the still, small voice of the Lord, from the Bible, a book, a bird, a 300-pound New York City firefighter, or a stranger we encounter on the road, "when the student is ready, the teacher appears." Certainly, the awesome God we serve has more than 10,000 instructors.

Another one of God's unexpected instructors appeared to Jean and me as we were serving as children's church ministers in 1985. Our children's church at New Life in Christ in Tampa was just that...it was "church"! It wasn't a babysitting service.

Jean and I claimed God's promise that He is no respecter of persons. We taught the kids God hears our prayers no matter how tall or small we are. Like hungry little sponges, these boys and girls took hold of God's promises and prayed in faith.

Our hearts were touched every Sunday as we would pray out loud with these King's kids about several issues. Without their parents knowing it, several kids began praying for their mom or dad to quit smoking. Soon, prayers of thanks were going up as each one of the parents put down their smokes!

One little four-year-old boy named Arthur would break our hearts with his prayers. "Dear Lord, help my daddy come back home to Mommy and me," he would pray week after week.

Arthur's dad was in the Air Force. He had left his wife and moved in with another woman. The handwriting on the wall convinced us this marriage was over.

The apparent hopelessness of the situation made little Arthur's prayers sound painfully futile. Undaunted, Arthur continued to pray the same prayer week after week.

These pitiful pleas persisted until one bright Sunday morning in children's church, Arthur prayed with what sounded like an "I told you so" kind of faith. "Thank You, Jesus, for sending my daddy home!"

That same night, in our living room, Jean and me, Arthur, and Arthur's mom and dad joined hands in a small circle. Arthur led us in an unforgettable prayer of thanks. "Oh, thank You, Jesus, for bringing my daddy home."

The psalmist reminds us, "Through the praise of children and infants you have established a stronghold against your enemies, to silence the foe and the avenger" (Psalm 8:2).

Arthur taught us that God makes a way where there appears to be no way. Truly. Our God is a way-making, life-changing, attitude-rearranging, fear & bondage-busting God, and He loves us with an everlasting love! There is nothing, absolutely nothing, impossible with God.

Yes! Paul was right. We may, indeed, have 10,000 instructors. However, we must be listening to recognize some are disguised as big strong firefighters. Others may come in the form of a broken-hearted four-year-old little boy.

Jesus said, "Whoever has ears, let them hear" (Matthew 11:15).

# Faith Challenge Questions

- Who has been an instructor or mentor in your walk with the Lord?

- What truths/revelations have they shared that you have adopted as your own?

- What has the Holy Spirit whispered to your heart?

- When was the last time you prayed with someone in need?

# CHAPTER SEVEN:

# PURPOSEFUL GRACE

*"The very quality of your life, whether you love it or
hate it, is based upon how thankful you
are toward God."*

**Francis Frangipane**

One of the foundational truths to our ministry and in
our personal walk of faith is found in Ephesians 2:8–10:

> *For it is by grace you have been saved,
> through faith—and it is not from yourselves,
> it is a gift of God—not by works, so that no
> one can boast. For we are God's handiwork,
> created in Christ Jesus to do good works,
> which God prepared in advance for us to do.*

This powerful truth brings such emphasis to two
essential ingredients of a healthy walk as a Christ-
follower. First, we are saved by grace! There is nothing
we can do to earn favor with God. As the old acronym

illustrates, grace is God's Riches At Christ's Expense.

Many a book has been written, and many a sermon has been preached on the amazing grace of God. However, in my forty-plus years of walking with Jesus, I have not heard much about how we respond to this awesome grace of God.

We usually hear the grace message in a way that confirms our salvation and reassures us that our sins are truly forgiven. But, as my old friends at Jews for Jesus in New York would say, "So what?" In other words, so what does this mean? So, what should I do? So, what should I give? So, where should I go?

Back to the scripture, Ephesians 2:10. We are God's "workmanship." A better translation is that we are God's "masterpiece." The word, masterpiece comes from the Greek word, *poema*. It's where we get our word, "poem."

Furthermore, Paul makes it abundantly clear this awesome grace by which we are saved is not a ticket we get punched and put in our back pocket.

This grace is purposeful. If we truly are recipients of God's incredible grace, we will be compelled to respond in some way, shape, or form.

I often say, "We don't work for grace. We work from grace, but we work!"

Therein is the second pearl found in this scripture! Now, I am not talking about dead or religious works, which will all certainly be burned up as stumble on that day (1 Corinthians 13:3). I am saying those who have been so blessed to have the mystery of the ages, namely Christ in us, revealed (Colossians 1:27), will rejoice in the work He calls us to.

Will it all be peaches and cream? No. There will be good days and bad days, good times and challenges. But we will have an inner joy that the world can't give and the world can't take away. This is what Scripture calls "the witness of the spirit."

Gold medalist turned missionary Eric Liddell once said, "God made me fast. And when I run, I feel His pleasure." Such is the actualized grace of God. It is not a theological position to be espoused but rather a life to be lived, a race to be run, a song to be sung.

When we park on Ephesians 2:8 and don't combine it with the call to action found in Ephesians 2:10, we shortchange the grace of God.

As I mentioned earlier, someone once said, "If you want to make God laugh, tell Him *your* plans."

It took me years to realize some of my marching orders would bring us into a dozen prisons in Florida, one in North Carolina, and two in Honduras. Who would have ever guessed that was part of God's Jeremiah 29:11 plan for us? Certainly not I!

During one of our ministry outreaches to death row in Starke, Florida, we were surprised as part of our day was redirected. We checked in with the chaplain's office as we always did, only to find there was a shakedown going on in the 330 cells that make up death row, or "condemned row," as the sign over that part of the prison reads.

The chaplain said we would be welcome to walk down the row after lunch, but it was off-limits all morning.

"You are certainly welcome to go on over to C-Dorm if you like." Sounded like a God assignment to my friend Larry and me, so off to C-Dorm we went.

Well, as I mentioned, with over twenty-five years of prison ministry in more than a dozen prisons, there is not much in the prison environment I am unfamiliar with. Yet, nothing could have prepared us for what we experienced that morning at C-Dorm at Union Correctional.

The moment the guards opened the metal door and allowed us access into C-Dorm, our ears were assaulted with the loud cries and curses of scores of men. Each man was locked in their own six-by-eight-foot cell.

These cells had cinderblock walls, no windows, and a thick metal door with only a four-inch by twenty-four-inch window in the door.

The anguished cries we heard walking into C-Dorm were the closest thing to Hades I have ever heard. The pain and rage that permeated the atmosphere were palpable.

Larry and I stuck our faces up to the door window of the first cell only to witness a young black man literally bouncing himself off the cinder block walls in his cell.

Underneath the window was a metal tray-like contraption the guards used to slide the prisoner's meals to them. Without understanding exactly why, except to somehow gain the prisoner's attention, I began banging my hand loudly on this metal contraption and, at the top of my lungs, yelled, "We're not religious; we just love Jesus!"

No doubt these inmates hadn't seen a visitor in God only knows how long. My banging caught the attention of the young prisoner, and he quit throwing himself into the walls.

He came to the thick glass strip of a window, and I repeated myself, "We're not religious; we just love Jesus." And I added, "Do you know Jesus loves you right where you are?"

The inmate's demeanor changed with a nod of affirmation, and he said something which so shocked me I will never forget it. He said, "I know...I was a worship leader in my church!"

In my flabbergasted state, I responded without even thinking. I said, "You're a worship leader? Do you know you have the power inside of you to change the atmosphere of this entire dorm?"

I began banging on the metal meal shelf on his door as if it were a drum and said, "Let's sing."

Against the backdrop of all the awful noise, Larry and I began singing as loud as we could, "Soon and very soon, we are going to see the King!" Our new worship leader friend began to join us, and the strangest thing happened.

With the suddenly of a waiter dropping a tray full of dishes in a noisy, crowded restaurant, everything went silent. The worship was so out of place everyone in the building went from screaming and cursing to listening in silence. There was an immediate and profound shift in the atmosphere.

In this newfound short-lived silence, Larry and I went to each one of the ugly metal cell doors and yelled the good news through to the prisoners. Seven men received Christ in C-Dorm that morning. As we walked by our worship leader's cell on the way out of C-Dorm, we could hear our friend was still worshipping. Muffled though it was, from all the metal and cinder blocks, we could clearly hear him singing, "The Center of My Joy."

Yes, God's grace is not an intellectual ascent or merely a theological talking point. God's grace is alive and active. It is full of purpose and promise and not without effect.

"We are saved by grace through faith" (Ephesians 2:8) (paraphrased by the author). Grace and faith are action words! If they are genuine, they provoke a response as natural as a sunrise.

While serving as an associate pastor at Freedom Ministries in Tampa, I inadvertently engaged in a lively, almost contentious debate one day with one of our twenty-four homeless residents who lived at the church.

Melvin had earned a master's degree in English. He took great issue with my statement that "faith was a verb." He ferociously defended his position that "faith was a noun."

After much discussion, we agreed that correct grammar would suggest faith is a noun, but good theology sees faith as a verb. James said, "Faith without action is dead." I say faith without action is not faith at all.

Sometimes we can be so focused on what we believe to be correct theology that we "strain a gnat and swallow a camel." If we are living a life that celebrates God's gifts, we will be too busy with our Father's business to argue over the different nuances of grace or faith.

I love what Philip Yancey says in his book, *What's So Amazing About Grace?* He says, "I would far rather convey grace than explain it."

One funny story I heard illustrates this pearl of wisdom better than I can. The story goes of a fishing village in Maine that was going through a dry spell. Almost all of the experienced fishermen were coming back to shore day after day without any fish. All that is except fisherman Jack.

Day after day, much to the dismay of his experienced onlookers, Jack was returning from his day at sea with a boatload of beautiful large fish.

This continued for several days until the veteran fisherman became suspicious. The concerned group convinced a local game warden to go out to sea with Jack for a day to see what was going on. Fisherman Jack welcomed his new guest, and off they went in Jack's boat to his favorite fishing spot several miles offshore.

After throwing out the nets, Jack reached under the dashboard, pulled out a stick of dynamite, lit it, and threw it in the ocean. After a mighty *bang*, dozens of large fish floated to the surface.

The game warden was beside himself as Jack brought the net full of fish onboard. He immediately began to read Jack the riot act. "You can't fish like that! This is dangerous, illegal, and unethical."

Before the dutiful game warden could conclude his rant, Jack handed the game warden another stick of dynamite. He lit the fuse and said, "Do you want to argue, or do you want to fish?"

So it often is with church leaders. We must repent of our foolish arguments and be about the business of becoming fishers of men and not keepers of the aquarium.

Another pearl from Yancey's *What's So Amazing About Grace?* illuminates one of our greatest needs: "We need 'grace-healed eyes' to see the potential in others for the same grace God has so lavishly bestowed upon us."

So, let me ask you a question. Do you want to argue, or do you want to fish? Just asking.

# Faith Challenge Questions

- How has your understanding of Grace morphed over the years?

- When have you been involved in an activity where you "felt God's pleasure"?

- How do you believe God wants you to respond to His grace?

- How has God's plan for your life been different than you thought it would be?

- When was the last time you were in a foolish argument? Did any good come from it?

# A Pearl of Spirit

## Love Was Wrapped

*"For the fruit of the Spirit is love"*
*(Galatians 5:22).*
**Love** *was wrapped up in a blanket*

*And placed within a manger;*

*Though the world was made by Him, He entered it a*
*stranger.*

**Joy** *in the person of Jesus*

*Came down from heaven above; He humbly entered the*
*Jordan*

*And was baptized with a dove.*

**Peace** *He is the Prince of,*

*He sought no earthly crown.*

*"No one takes My life from Me,*

*For I freely lay it down."*

**Patience** *was personified*

*As He faced the Roman whips;*

*Pilate's threats and curses*

*Brought silence from His lips.*

**Kindness** *He exemplified*

*As He hung between two thieves:*

*Amidst the nails and thorns, He pled,*

*"Father, forgive them, please."*

**Goodness** *was wrapped up in a blanket and placed in a borrowed grave.*

*Yet rose victorious on the third day; He died to make death His slave!*

**Faithfulness** *He promises to all who go His way,*

*So, seek ye first His kingdom on this holy Christmas day.*

**Gentleness** *a garment,*

*Given by the King of kings; wrap it tightly 'round thee*

*And hear all of heaven sing.*

**Self-control** *I've often found an elusive quality; The "me, myself, and I" must die*

*To be reborn on bended knee.*

*The manger, cross, and empty tomb.*

*The inseparable trinity;*

*All wrapped inside a simple man:*

*A man from Galilee.*

# CHAPTER EIGHT:

# SWEET SPOT OF GRACE

*"Believers, look up – take courage.*
*The angels are nearer than you think."*

**Billy Graham**

In his book, *In a Pit with a Lion on a Snowy Day*, author and pastor Mark Batterson gives fresh insight into a word commonly used in Christendom: "righteousness."

Batterson says, "We mistakenly think of righteousness as 'doing nothing wrong' when, in fact, righteousness is 'doing something right.' Righteousness isn't just running away from sin. Righteousness is chasing lions."

If you Google Mark Batterson and check out his testimony, you will find the man practices what he preaches.

His insight and emphasis regarding righteousness are refreshing and spot on. In seminary, we are taught "righteousness is right standing before God." Certainly, this is true. Scripture in 2 Corinthians 5:21 says, "God made him who had no sin to be sin for us, so that in him we might become the righteousness of God."

The best definition I have ever heard for success is "standing before God unashamed." One may ask, well, who could ever do that? I believe every single believer has that very opportunity. One day each one of us will stand before God, and the books will be opened. Will we hear those words, "Well done" or "Well, it's done"?

Regarding our sin and shame, which were all taken care of in full on the cross. So, how do we respond to such sacrificial love? What is our responsibility? Don't you love that word, "responsibility"? When I look at that word, I see two words: response and ability. God has given each of us the ability to respond. Now your response will and certainly should be different from mine.

Thank God not everyone is called to serve as a pastor or prison minister. The truth be told, unless you are compelled to serve in these capacities, you would be wise to run from such undertakings faster than Joseph ran from Potiphar's wife.

One of the pearls I have discovered in my journey deals with finding one's purpose and call. In Japanese culture, this is referred to as "ikigai," meaning "your purpose in life." In ikigai, one's purpose is found at the intersection of what you are good at and what you love. I like that a lot. We will look more closely at ikigai a little later.

One sure way to find out what you are good at and what you love is by trying different things. As you do, you will discover your passion and gifts, and your gift will make way for you (Proverbs 18:16).

When we go where the Lord says, "Go," and do what the Lord says, "Do," we will walk in a fullness of joy and a knowing that we are realizing our purpose. I call it walking in the sweet spot of God's grace.

Personally, I believe only Jesus walked in perfect step with the Holy Spirit (John 5). The rest of us are, in a sense, stumbling to glory. However, as we walk by faith and not by sight, we catch glimpses of His glory, which keep us moving in the right direction.

I know the old saying is true; we are "human beings" and not "human doings," but what on earth are we here for? Or, as I heard one preacher preach, "Don't just do something, stand there!" Yes, there is a time and place to practice Psalm 46:10 and "be still and know that He is God." There is also a time to "pick up our cross and follow Him."

As we grow in our awareness of who we are in Christ, we discover God does have a plan for our life, a very personal, unique plan that only we can fulfill.

Richard Foster is spot on in his book, *Celebration of Discipline*. He says, "Spiritual direction is first born out of natural spontaneous human relationships." God often works through people. Our purpose is revealed in those things we are most passionate about.

My hands-down all-time favorite movie is, *It's a Wonderful Life*. In this old classic, which still airs on network TV during the Christmas season, actor Jimmy Stewart plays the part of struggling building and loan owner George Bailey.

Through unforeseen calamity, George Bailey's uncle, Billy, loses all the building and loan money. George's life and livelihood spin out of control in a downward spiral until he is standing on a bridge on the brink of suicide.

A goofy angel by the name of Clarence shows up and, to save George, grants him his wish that he would "never be born." Much of the movie deals with how very different George's friends, family, and community would be if George had never existed.

Towards the end of the movie, George cries out to God for help. "Please, God, I want to live again." God restores George's life with a renewed perspective and gratitude. One might say George is born again with a heightened awareness of how precious of a gift life is. The movie does a great job of illustrating how the tapestry of our lives interwoven with the lives of others in ways we are not even aware of.

It really is a wonderful life each of us has been given. God really does answer prayer. His angels are real, and thank God they are not goofy clumsy angels like Clarence in *It's a Wonderful Life*. Scripture teaches us that "angels [are] ministering spirits sent to serve those who will inherit salvation" (Hebrews 1:14).

These mighty messengers of God help us in our journey with Jesus more than we are aware. In his first epistle (no, the "epistles" were not the wives of the "apostles"), John the Beloved says in 1 John 4:17, "In this world we are like Jesus." When we study the life and ministry of Jesus, we recognize the huge role angels played in His life to help fulfill Jesus' purpose and call.

At the incarnation, we are privileged to sit in on a conversation between Mary and Gabriel. Before His birth, Joseph is visited by an angel in his sleep, letting Joseph know the legitimacy of Mary's claim of who Jesus is. Also, before Jesus is born, Jesus' relative, Zechariah (the father of John the Baptist), is visited by an angel.

At Jesus' birth, we see a whole angelic choir show up and sing "Glory to God in the highest." Angels then intervene and direct Joseph and Mary to move in a different direction, saving their lives from certain peril. During Jesus' temptation in the wilderness, Scripture tells us that "an angel from heaven appeared to him and strengthened him" (Luke 22:43). More angels come and strengthen Jesus as He sweats blood in the Garden of Gethsemane. There in the garden, Jesus tells Peter, "Do you think I cannot call on my Father, and he will at once put at my disposal more than twelve legions of angels?" (Matthew 26:53).

At the empty tomb, angels question Mary and ask, "Why do you look for the living among the dead?" (Luke 24:5). Immediately after Jesus' ascension, angels question Jesus' disciples, asking why they are staring at the sky, and reassuring them Jesus will return one day. Finally, in the book of Revelation, we see a picture of Jesus' return with innumerable angels! Don't you love that word, innumerable? Webster defines the word innumerable as "too many to be counted"!

My point is—and this is certainly a pearl of truth to be cherished—if what John said is true, and we truly are "like Him in this world," wouldn't it be obvious that God's angels are at work in our lives as well? As a matter of fact, in Hebrews 13:2, the author warns us to "not forget to show hospitality to strangers, for by so doing some people have shown hospitality to angels without knowing it."

No, we don't worship angels, but we don't ignore them either. They are very real, and more are those who are with us than those (demons) who are against us. Angels intervened for Peter in Acts 12 and worked on behalf of Daniel in Daniel 10, and they are at work in our lives also.

Consider God's friend, Elisha, and his servant as they were under attack by the army of the king of Aram (2 Kings 6). They were surrounded by warriors in chariots who had strict orders to capture them. As his servant began to panic, Elisha prayed for the Lord to open his eyes. The faithful servant looked and saw his would-be captors surrounded by chariots of fire! God's angels intervened and prevented their certain demise.

Six-time Grammy-winning contemporary Christian recording artist, Amy Grant, wrote a song in 1984 called "Angels." She performed it during the 1985 Grammy awards, where she received a Grammy for Best Gospel

Vocal Performance. Amy's "Angels" song does a fabulous job suggesting the myriad of times angels protect us without our even knowing.

Knowing God is for us, His angels surround us, His Spirit is alive within us (1 Corinthians 6:17; Colossians 1:27; 1 John 4:4), He hears our prayers and honors our study of His Scriptures (2 Timothy 2:15), we can boldly come before His throne of grace and ask Him to lead us (Romans 8:14) and reveal His will for our lives (Romans 12:1–2).

Mark Batterson's definition of true righteousness is a good one! When we are walking in the light as Jesus is in the light, we are moved by His Spirit to go where Jesus says, "Go," and do what Jesus says, "Do."

We discover God's unique personal plan and call for our lives "as we go." God will not steer a parked car!

# Faith Challenge Questions

- How do you describe righteousness?

- Can you recall catching a glimpse of God's glory?

- How does God direct your steps?

- How aware are you of God's angels?

- What is your primary passion in life?

# A Pearl of Fire

## Chariots of Fire

*"He looked and saw the hills full of horses and
chariots of fire" (2 Kings 6:17).*

*Chariots of angelic fire*
*Encamped about the town*
*Chosen before earth's creation*
*For a king without a crown.*
*Shadowed by a painful cross*
*The humble stable proudly stood*
*As a lighthouse for the blind,*
*Birthing hope through a manger of wood.*
*God so loved, He sent His Son*
*To show us once He was grown*
*"Let you who be without a sin*
*Be the first to throw a stone."*
*The grace-filled Lamb of God,*
*The embodiment of love;*
*"I've come to do not my will,*
*But that of my Father above."*
*Chariots of angelic fire*
*Encamped about the town*

*Chosen before earth's creation*
*For a king with a thorny crown.*
*"Abba, Father, please forgive them!"*
*Cried our Lord, the Prince of Peace.*
*"This day you'll be in paradise,"*
*He promised a common thief.*
*In joyful, heavenly splendor*
*It was finished; it was done:*
*The precious babe of Bethlehem*
*Over sin, the battle won.*
*Rejoice, oh earth, this Christmas Day:*
*Not by works but by His grace.*
*God has chariots of angelic fire*
*For all who seek His face!*

# CHAPTER NINE:

# LIFE-CHANGING KEPHALE

*"Whoever is happy will make others happy too."*

**Anne Frank**

Have you learned not to compare yourself or your call with others? As we grow in our awareness of Christ in us, we become more and more aware that God has created us to be unique. He has a tailor-made plan for each of us. Do we miss it from time to time? Of course, we do. However, if we seek first His kingdom and His righteousness, He works "all things" together for our good because we love Him and are called according to His purposes.

As I mentioned, we often discover God's plan by trial and error. More specifically, our errors can result in many trials! Some of the pearls we uncover can come with an expensive price tag. Like many things, I learned this the hard way.

Jean and I were married in 1976 and radically saved in 1979. As I was in prayer one morning soon after we came to faith, I heard the Lord say, "You will live in Florida." We were living in North Carolina at the time.

As soon as I heard this still, small voice, I started walking to our front door. Jean asked, "Where are you going?" Not missing a step, I said, "I'm going to Winn Dixie to get some boxes to pack...we're moving to Florida."

At this point in our marriage, we were not a part of a church and knew nothing about seeking counsel from older and wiser believers for major life decisions. We both believed "the husband was the boss," so my declaration wasn't open for debate or discussion. If Forest Gump had weighed in on my decision, he no doubt would have surmised, "Stupid is as stupid does!"

Jean and our two precious children, Connie & Jimmy, moved in with my in-laws in New York. I drove to Tampa (that night!) and moved in with my aunt and uncle. I got a job at 84 Lumber and began working a sixty-hour workweek in hopes of saving enough money to rent our own place.

It's hot in Florida in July and August. After six weeks of my foolhardy plan, I couldn't stand being away from my family any longer and moved in with Jean and our kids in my in-laws' two-and-a-half-bedroom apartment in Long Island City, New York.

Four years before, we rocked my father-in-law's

world with our unexpected pregnancy. Now, we were back! To say this experience was humbling would be the understatement of the century.

In his book, *The Three Battlegrounds*, Francis Frangipane says, "Whatever lofty spiritual plane you imagine that you are on, remember: Adam was in Paradise when he fell." God has His ways of humbling us if we do not humble ourselves.

Soon, I was working hard as a busboy and then as a waiter in Manhattan. It took about six months to save up enough money to get on our feet, with our own place. God blessed our lives in many ways over the next four years.

One unexpected blessing came in the way of our apartment building "going co-op." This happens when the owner of the building decides to sell the apartments. This resulted in our being offered a payment of $8,333 if we agreed not to renew our lease.

I had never been released from what I heard the Lord tell me: "You will live in Florida." So, with this unexpected windfall combined with the money we had already saved, we packed up and moved to the Sunshine State.

We received precious pearls of wisdom through this excursion through the wilderness. One important pearl is recognizing the importance of husbands and wives learning to "submit one to another."

Any marriage that has a domineering spouse is headed for trouble. Take it from me. I know this is true because I was "that guy." If you are a young husband reading this book, please hit the pause button right here and do a word study on the little Greek word, *"kephale."*

Don't take my word for it; study it for yourself. Be like the Bereans we read about in Acts 17:11,

> *The Berean Jews were of more noble character than those in Thessalonica, for they received the message with great eagerness and examined the Scriptures every day to see if what Paul said was true.*

This little Greek word, *kephale*, shattered some painful misconceptions I had for years about marriage. In Scripture, when Paul speaks of the husband being the "head" of the wife, he uses the word *"kephale."* This speaks to the husband being like a riverhead or source of life to his wife. It directly contradicts any suggestion of the man being "the boss" over the woman.

*Our wedding day, Dec. 17, 1976*

As I'm writing this, Jean and I are in our forty-sixth year of marriage. Discovering the pearl of *"kephale"* took place about fifteen years ago. It was more than a game-changer; it was a life and ministry changer. We are much happier and healthier today because of discovering this one little pearl of great value.

In his book, *Discovering the Heart of a Man*, author and marriage counselor Ken Nair says: "Ignorance about God's concepts and purposes for man and woman causes misunderstanding and fear." Amen to that!

Nair also hits the nail on the head when he says, "A

wife is usually more in touch with her husband's spirit than he is." Humbling but true.

Jean and I faced many challenges and worked through many difficulties in our more than two decades of serving in full-time ministry. The truth be told, for many reasons, ministry is hard on marriage.

During times of struggle, I would think, *If I could just get closer to the Holy Spirit, I could be a better husband to Jean.* One of the surprising discoveries I made was, "as I get closer to Jean's spirit, I find myself closer and more yielded to God's Holy Spirit."

As a guy, intimacy with the Holy Spirit did not come quickly or easily for me. I mean, who has the time? As the late great Harry Chapin put it in his classic song, "Cat's in the Cradle," "There were planes to catch, and bills to pay. He learned to walk while I was away."

Whether we are talking about quality relationships with our kids, our spouse, or God's Holy Spirit, we must exercise those "four L's" we mentioned from *Kairos*; "listen, listen, love, love." If we are too busy to cultivate a first love relationship with Holy Spirit, we are too busy.

In his *Discovering the Heart of a Man*, Ken Nair says, "In order to help a man learn, could not a wife be an agent of Holy Spirit?" Lord knows my wife Jean has been that "Holy Spirit helper" in my life, and I have no doubt I am closer to Him because of her. Please don't tell her. Let this be our secret. LOL.

The second valuable pearl is that "plans fail for lack

of counsel" (Proverbs 15:22). If we had been a part of a Christian community at the time I decided to "go to Winn Dixie," we could have been spared a world of pain and problems.

Being in a relationship with other older, more experienced believers doesn't mean we become mindless robots. However, as Bob Dylan once said, "You're gonna have to serve somebody. Well, it may be the devil or it may be the Lord, but you're gonna have to serve somebody."

We have discovered serving in the church is both a joy and a privilege. I love what John Bevere says in his book, *Honor's Reward*. He says, "It's all about serving in the Kingdom, and when we honor one another, each of us is more effective in pleasing God." So true.

For me, it took a real attitude adjustment to look at the Christian community as a place of safety and shelter. Again, John Bevere brings truth to light in his *Honor's Reward* by saying, "Submission deals with our attitude, whereas obedience is related to our actions."

Zig Ziglar coined the catchy phrase, "Your attitude determines your altitude." I don't know about you, but for me, developing and maintaining a positive attitude, especially when working with difficult or negative people, is not always easy.

Will we cultivate and display a positive attitude or a negative attitude? Each morning each of us makes a choice to either greet the new day by saying, "Good morning, Lord," or by saying, "Good Lord, it's morning."

It's a choice we make.

As we go through our individual journey, every one of us faces many situations where we must choose to light a candle or curse the darkness.

Some ask, "Is the glass half-full or half-empty?" As I was praying about that age-old question one day, I heard the Lord answer me. He said, "It depends if the glass is being filled or being emptied!"

In Ephesians 5:18, Paul tells us to be "filled with the Spirit." As you study that out, you will find what he is really saying is, "Be being filled with the Spirit."

When we cultivate a first love relationship with Jesus, we will walk in a consistent place of refilling. Because we all leak in many ways, we need that constant refilling to stay positive.

We have discovered those individuals who are positive and speak well of others are often people of great integrity. Those poor negative souls who speak poorly of others will speak poorly of you as soon as your back is turned.

In her book, *Switch on Your Brain*, Dr. Caroline Leaf says, "Science shows us we are wired for love with a natural optimism bias."

One positive person of true integrity who blessed our life was a tall redhead by the name of May. Back in her day, May was a network news anchor and a skydiver who used to fly from time to time with The Blue Angels flight demonstration squadron.

Little did I know when I first met May, she would

become a lifelong friend and the oldest person to graduate from our Higher Ground School of Ministry.

May came into our world in the early 1990s as I was working as director of corporate support at PBS's Tampa affiliate, WEDU TV. May was pitching an idea for a children's music program. As she and I drove from Tampa to Miami to pitch her show to Blockbuster Video, May talked and talked about how much she loved Jesus, her husband, and her pastor Bill.

*May & Bill Moseley on their wedding day*

When we planted our church in 1999, May and her husband were our very first ministry partners. Over the next twenty years, May sent a note of encouragement and a love gift every single month without fail.

As well as ministering in the women's jail in Cumberland County, Tennessee, May was the number one pen pal to my death row friend, Manny Valle, until the day of his execution.

May went to heaven a few months ago. Even in her late eighties, she was a committed and classy Christian lady who always spoke well of others.

Although May was a student and ultimately a graduate of our Higher Ground School of Ministry, she was also one of God's special ambassadors who taught us and everyone she encountered the power of a positive, loving spirit.

John Wesley once said, "Do all the good you can, in all the ways you can, to all the souls you can, in every place you can, at all the times you can, with all the zeal you can, as long as ever you can."

Our friend May was that kind of person.

# Faith Challenge Questions

- When was the last time you received an unexpected blessing?

- Do you wake up and say, "Good morning, Lord," or "Good Lord, it's morning"?

- Do you usually see the glass "half-empty" or "half-full"?

# A Pearl of Grace

## The Man from Galilee

*"Jesus returned to Galilee in the power*
*of the Spirit" (Luke 4:14).*

*There was a man from Galilee*
*Who fed the poor and calmed the sea.*
*He healed the sick and raised the dead:*
*He's a blasphemer, the wise men said.*
*From His mother's holy womb,*
*Yes, even after the empty tomb*
*Joseph wondered and the apostles too:*
*Lord Jesus Christ, is it really You?*
*Thirty-three years went rolling by*
*Before our Lord Jesus was told to die.*
*Father, oh Father, please take this death bed.*
*But not my will, Father, Your will instead.*
*It was in that garden,*
*Where He sweated and prayed,*
*The Lord Jesus Christ*
*Was soon betrayed.*
*They whipped Him and beat Him*
*Yes, they killed Him, too.*
*Did you know that He died*

*For me and for you?*
*There was a man from Galilee*
*Who fed the poor and calmed the sea*
*And when it all is said and done.*
*You, too, will know that He's the one.*
*I hear the gates to hell are wide*
*And I want to see you on the other side.*
*Oh, listen, please listen, is that a trumpet I hear?*
*Oh, listen, please listen, Judgment Day is so near!*
*So listen and read,*
*Be humbled and pray*
*For it is His promise,*
*You, too, will soon say:*
*"Praise Jesus of Nazareth;*
*Thank You, dear Lord."*
*Yes, Jesus of Nazareth:*
*Jesus is Lord!*

# CHAPTER TEN:

# SENSING GOD'S PLEASURE

*"Your talent is God's gift to you."*

**Leo Buscaglia**

What are your gifts?

Are you exercising and developing them?

Are you using your gifts to bless others?

Do you have a teaching gift? Then teach.

Do you have a singing gift? Then sing.

Do you have a dancing gift? Then dance.

Do you have a praying gift? Then pray.

Do you have a serving gift? Then serve.

Do you have a giving gift? Then give.

Do you have a writing gift? Then write.

Start where you are. Be faithful with the little. Commit

your gifts to the Lord. Don't compare yourself to others. Stick with it. Don't allow the devil or Job's counselors to discourage you. Do what you do to bless the Lord and others, and it will grow.

Perhaps you are like many people we encounter who started to develop their gifts and quit. So many of God's people have beautiful gifts sitting on the shelf, gathering dust. Somewhere along the way, they got discouraged or became complacent.

Proverbs 22:6 says, "Start children off on the way they should go, and even when they are old they will not turn from it."

If someone had shared the pearl hidden in this verse, I would have been a better dad. You see, I thought this meant to "train a child" to be honest, work hard, do well in school, go to college, get a good job, etc.

Our daughter, Connie, did just that. As a *cum laude* graduate from the University of South Florida and a P. E. teacher, Connie had no trouble landing a job and excelling in her field.

Connie was always wonderful at working with kids and gifted in creating fun, effective object lessons. She is a gifted teacher. Those same gifts are now being exercised as she and her husband, Steven, pastor our church with joy and excellence.

Our son, Jimmy, never had an interest in college. Jimmy joined the Army right after high school and graduated from his basic combat training with honors.

After his honorable discharge, he married his high school sweetheart and started a family. Jimmy and Melissa now own and operate three thriving businesses, have a beautiful family, a beautiful home, a boat, new cars, and serve faithfully as associate pastors at our church.

Back to the proverb. Not many years ago, someone explained in Hebrew that this scripture is really saying to train or raise your child "according to their bending."

What better parents we all would be if we would recognize and help cultivate the unique gift and passion within our children rather than try to impose what we think is right for them.

In his *Honor's Reward*, John Bevere says, "The leader displays his or her honor toward the team members by praising their efforts."

Words have power. It's a beautiful thing when words are used to affirm and build others up, be it in the faith or in particular gifting.

Many grow up in a negative atmosphere where positive words of affirmation are not found. Since she was a kid, my wife Jean loved to dance. When she was fifteen years old, she convinced her parents to pay twenty dollars a month to attend a local dance school.

A year later, at the big dance recital, the class tap danced to a lively patriotic song. Jean and her fellow dancers gave their all. Afterward, her dad's only comment was, "Two hundred bucks for that?" Those cruel words pierced her heart. Discouraged but not defeated, Jean kept dancing.

Many years later, Jean discovered Christian interpretive dance. She joined an interpretive dance team led by a very talented and experienced dance leader. Although her instructor was a great dancer, she offered Jean no encouragement. As a matter of fact, she told Jean she "had two left feet" and most likely wouldn't be able to dance with the team. Boy, was she wrong?

Jean did not give up on her passion. She worked all the harder and developed the gift she knew was inside of her. She and her interpretive dance team, Wings of Praise, have danced before thousands in the packed Ocean Center in Daytona Beach and on GOD TV…. They have ushered in the Holy Spirit in church services, large and small, in prisons and on the mission fields of Honduras.

Perhaps what is most admirable is how Jean has shared her gift and passion with others. Wings of Praise dance team now has three generations of anointed dancers, all because that little discouraged teenage tap dancer didn't give up on the gift she knew was inside of her. Jean is now sixty-five years young, and, praise God, she is still "kickin'" with the twenty-year-olds!

Remember the quote we shared by Olympic Gold Medalist Eric Liddell? "God made me fast. And when I run, I feel His pleasure." Well, God made Jean graceful and passionate, and when she dances, we all sense God's pleasure.

As I mentioned, we recently discovered a little Japanese word that can change your life. The word is *"ikigai."* The meaning of *"ikigai"* is "finding joy in life through purpose." In other words, your *"ikigai"* is what gets you up in the morning, your reason for being.

The Japanese concept of *"ikigai"* includes finding what you love and how to get paid for it. Confucius put it this way, "Choose a job you love, and you won't have to work a day in your life."

Since she was a little girl, my sister, Tica, loved fashion. Tica's love for fashion and her good looks served her quite well through her college years. Much of her college tuition was paid by scholarships she received by winning beauty pageants.

*My big sister, Tica Tallent*

Along the way to earning her master's degree in education, Tica won a number of beauty crowns: Miss Peach Festival; Miss Watermelon Festival; Miss Piedmont;

Miss Columbia, and a number of other titles.

Although Tica was a gifted teacher and taught second grade for ten years, she never lost her passion for fashion. One of Tica's three published books is entitled, *What is Beautiful*.

With her unique gift of graceful tenacity, Tica successfully sold a leading department store on the idea of creating a position for her to be paid as their "Personal Shopper."

It was a win-win. The department store benefitted from Tica's knowledge of fashion and excellent people skills, and Tica took great delight in helping her clients look their best with just the right styles and color combinations.

For more than a decade, this unique synergy resulted in Tica working with scores of young women with a community outreach program called the "Teen Board." Along with participating in their annual fashion show, these young ladies found a loving, caring mentor as they enjoyed quality time with Tica.

Tica's love for fashion didn't gather dust on the shelf. Her passion moved her to action, and she found her "*ikigai*"—her joyful purpose—helping others while doing what she loved.

# Faith Challenge Questions

- What are you passionate about?

- What are your kids passionate about?

- When have you sensed God's pleasure?

- What gifts in you have become dormant?

# A Pearl of Mercy

## They're Beautiful

*"To the pure, all things are pure"* (Titus 1:15).

New Jersey is known as the Garden State. That's where I was born. That's where I grew up. It wasn't unusual for the homes in our neighborhood to have beautiful gardens all around them. Our home was unusual in many ways. However, in this one regard, our home was not different from most. Our front yard was the home of three gardens.

To teach us responsibility and that work was more than just a four-letter word, my dad assigned each of those gardens to the care of my two sisters and me. Each of us had our own garden. For a five-year-old boy, that was a pretty big deal! My eldest sister, Tica, cared for the largest garden. Like Tica, it was always beautiful and well-groomed. Roxie's garden was smaller than Tica's but larger than mine. Perhaps fitting for the middle child, Roxie's seemed to be the most colorful. I was the baby in the family. My garden was a long row of tulips that ran alongside the house. Sometimes my friend K. J. and I would catch a mess of fish down at Deefy Leaves and bury them in the garden as fertilizer. Many Saturdays, while we were raking the yard or tending the garden, we would watch our friends riding by on their bicycles. As a kid, I resented my dad making us work in the yard. As a man, I'm so thankful he did. He gave each of us his work ethic.

One spring morning, I found myself wandering around the house, looking for something to do. I noticed that my tulip garden was in full bloom. I thought to myself, *I bet Mommy would like these flowers.* So I took a pair of scissors and cut every one of those tulips right under the flower, destroying the entire garden. I gathered up the pile of tulip tops in the makeshift pouch I had created with my T-shirt and brought them into the house. "Mommy, I brought you a present," I shouted as I walked into the house. In a glimpse, my mom surmised exactly what had just taken place. She paused a moment and then exclaimed, "They're beautiful!" She then filled a large crystal bowl with water and lovingly placed the floating tulip tops on the dining room table. It wasn't until many years later that I realized what a special gift I had been given. Today I understand what James, the brother of Jesus, meant when he said, "Mercy triumphs over judgment" (James 2:13b).

Mom, well, she went to help Jesus "prepare a place for us." When we get there, I won't be a bit surprised if my sisters and I don't find tulip tops floating in the Crystal Sea. Thanks, Mom.

# CHAPTER ELEVEN:

# GOD MAKES A WAY

*"Never succumb to the temptation of bitterness."*
**Dr. Martin Luther King**

So, what's your heart's desire?

In the last chapter, we talked about purpose and fulfillment and that little powerful Japanese word, *"ikigai,"* finding our purpose in that which gives us joy. This philosophy is worth carefully considering.

However, if we are honest with ourselves, we must admit there is a mystery between the sovereignty of God and the free will of man. It is one of the age-old debates in church history. Did God choose man, or does man choose God? Perhaps the answer to both is "yes"!

How much of our life has been ordered by the Lord before we are born, and how much of our life experience is a result of making good choices while developing and exercising a good work ethic? Certainly, many people don't plan to fail; they simply fail to plan. The result of that lackadaisical approach to life is often riddled with mediocrity and a lackluster journey through a maze of life's obstacles, challenges, and disappointments.

Yet, on the flip side of the "failing to plan coin" is the pearl of revelation, which brings a smile not because it's funny but because it's true. Namely, "If you want to make God laugh, tell Him your plans!" This I know full well.

One day when I was twelve years old, I ran into my grandmother's house after playing outside. She stopped me in my tracks and asked, "Jimmy, when you grow up, do you think you will be a minister like your grandfather?" I had no interest in the ministry whatsoever. She may as well have asked me if I planned to one day walk on the moon.

Fast forward forty years, and even as I was serving in ministry, I never imagined I would be involved in prison ministry. I was wholeheartedly convinced "that" kind of ministry was for other people and certainly not for me.

Yet, God has a way of making a way, and as we grow in surrender, Proverbs 3:5 becomes more and more a reality in our day-to-day living. "Trust in the Lord with all your heart and lean not on your own understanding; in all your ways submit to him, and he will make your paths straight."

There is much I don't understand about the workings and timings of God, but there is a pearl I have discovered in my later years that will bless and help you if you take hold of it. Regardless of which side of the debate you lean on concerning the sovereignty of God and the free will of man debate, there is one thing for certain. God is not in a hurry!

Consider Moses, who, after killing an Egyptian, spent forty years on the backside of a desert before having his burning bush encounter.

Consider Noah, who worked tirelessly with his family for more than one hundred years building that ark without a drop of rain falling.

Consider Joshua. Yes, we love to talk about Joshua and Caleb as mighty men of valor who were the only two of the twelve spies exploring the promised land who had faith and gave Moses a good report. Oh, how we love to quote Joshua's powerful words from Joshua 1:9: "Be strong and courageous. Do not be afraid."

However, if we rewind the tape and ask where Joshua was when Moses was trekking up Mt. Sinai to receive the ten commandments, we see Joshua melting down the jewelry of his friends and family to help make the golden calf!

No, God is not in a hurry!

The psalmist instructs us to "take delight in the Lord, and he will give you the desires of your heart" (Psalm 37:4). This one promise of Scripture sustained my friend, "Gator," as he served almost nineteen years of his forty-year sentence in prison.

Earlier, I shared a little about our good friend, Gator.

After more than a decade in prison, Gator found himself alone "in the box" (solitary confinement), contemplating his second homicide.

He had no Bible. There was no Christian music playing. There were no preachers or chaplains anywhere to be seen. It was just Gator and a belly full of anger when the Holy Spirit decided to invade his space. As the presence of God filled Gator's hot lonely cell, he wept for seven days.

After being released back into the general population, Gator made a beeline to the chaplain's office to share his supernatural encounter. Chaplain Dave, who has become a dear friend over the last twenty years of our ministering at Putnam Prison, said he "watched Gator like a hawk for six months" before he fully realized his transformation was genuine.

Now, Gator has been out of prison for almost as long as he was in prison, and this promise of God has surely come to pass in his life. He now has a godly wife, Kim. Together they enjoy good health, have good jobs, and a beautiful family. They love to vacation in their RV at their lakefront property. The icing on the cake is they both are thriving with a vibrant prison ministry.

Not only has Gator's conversion been as genuine as it is dramatic, but so it has been with Gator's victim's brother. As I shared, as soon as Gator killed his ex-wife, Vera, shooting her six times, his brother-in-law, Burt, heard about it. Burt grabbed his shotgun and went to find Gator. By the grace of God, the sheriff found him first.

For many years, Burt pledged he would one day avenge his sister's death. Burt even used Gator's expected release date as his PIN number. For more than a decade, every time Burt would use his PIN number, he would remind himself, "This is the date I will take Gator off the planet."

It's been said that harboring resentment is like drinking poison hoping the other guy will die. So, it was with Burt. For years his anger and resentment pushed him to drink and punch walls. There was more than one man in prison after Vera's murder. Gator's prison was made with bars. Burt's was made of hate.

Gator would have certainly received the death penalty had it not been for his victim's parents, who were committed Christians and fought against the death penalty.

A few years after the murder, Vera's mom forgave Gator. Seven years after the murder, Vera's dad (a Methodist pastor) forgave Gator.

I was so very blessed to spend some quality time with Vera's dad, Rev. B. With tears in his eyes, he shared, with tremendous humility and transparency, how he wrestled with the Lord for seven long agonizing years before forgiving Gator.

Not long before Gator's release, after many years of anguish, God got a hold of Vera's brother, Burt, and he forgave Gator also.

What the devil intended for evil, God has turned into something quite beautiful. This amazing true story of forgiveness and redemption was featured on The 700

Club. Gator and Burt now serve together on many *Kairos* Christian renewal weekends and at various churches and media outlets.

Understanding God is not in a hurry is not a bad thing. It is a good thing. When we look around and see, both in our lives and in the lives of those men and women in the Bible, we see God is not in a hurry. This simple, profound truth can help us realize God's ways are different than our ways, and His timing is different than ours. Learning to wait on the Lord is a pearl of discovery worth pursuing.

When I was a kid, I knew a girl who loved horses. I mean, she really loved horses. She would hang around Watchung Stables in Summit, New Jersey, just to be around horses every chance she could. She would literally shovel horse manure for an hour just to ride for half an hour. Now that's love!

As this girl grew into a young woman, she dreamed of owning her own horse one day. Yet, life has its way of keeping us busy with many things. Although this girl's love for animals was plain to see, getting married, becoming a mom, making a living, and all that life throws at you seemed to eclipse her childhood dream of one day having her own horse.

This young girl, Roxanne, grew to become an executive with the University of North Carolina's School of Family Medicine. After weathering the pains of divorce, she married again. Along with raising their three kids together, Roxie and her husband, Junior, served the youth at their church and helped support many mission trips and evangelistic outreaches.

Junior was interested in buying some jet skis and spending weekends on the lake. Yet, Junior was more interested in making his wife happy than he was in purchasing jet skis. "Happy wife, happy life!" (Now that's a pearl of discovery if I ever saw one!)

After this good man considered his wife's lifelong dream and desire to own a horse, they purchased two horses, and he learned to ride. They now live on an eleven-acre ranch in North Carolina with three horses and a dog. One or two weekends a month, they load up two of their horses into their horse trailer/camper and trek up to Uwharrie, North Carolina, to enjoy their cabin and go trail riding.

*Roxie & Junior trail riding in N.C.*

I have had a ringside seat to watch the desires of this girl's heart be fulfilled. You see, Roxanne (Roxie) is my sister. I assure you, watching Roxie's lifelong heart desires become a reality didn't happen overnight. However, Roxie & Junior are a couple who truly love the Lord, and God has blessed them in a profound way. They exemplify God's promise: "Take delight in the Lord, and he will give you the desires of your heart" (Psalm 37:4). God is faithful, but He's not in a hurry.

# Faith Challenge Questions

- Have you ever been poisoned by unforgiveness?

- How have you seen God bring good out of tragedy?

- Have you ever been impatient waiting on God?

- What are the desires of your heart?

# A Pearl of Time

## Beautiful Watches

*"My God will meet all your needs"*
*(Philippians 4:19).*

Canchias, Honduras, changed us. We arrived on a mission to teach but departed as students most blessed. Early one morning, our core team was graced with an unforgettable tour of this very poor village, where naked brown children and kind, toothless women greeted us at every turn. We discovered that the small dwellings with dirt floors and cut-out windows were more than huts. They were homes. Although the Canchians had no electricity or running water, they had each other and a remarkable, almost contagious, resilience.

Nancy lived in one of the small huts. She was five years old and had never worn a pair of shoes. Her smile eclipsed her surroundings as we placed new sandals on her feet.

We saw many humbling sights and met many precious souls in Canchias. Each one touched our hearts with a warmth only God could give.

At the end of our expedition, I asked our guide, "Of all the needs you have here in Canchias, what are your greatest needs?"

"Needs? We have no needs," he replied. "The Lord provides all of our needs. You Americans have beautiful watches, but you have no time!"

Later that afternoon, while building a church in a nearby town, my watch band broke. Not having the heart to repair it, I carried that watch in my pocket for the next two years. Whenever I reached into my pocket to check the time, I could see that Honduran man's smiling face, and I could hear his voice saying: "You Americans have beautiful watches, but you have no time!"

# CHAPTER TWELVE:

# A BLASTED PROTESTANT

*"Remember no one can make you feel inferior
without your consent."*

**Eleanor Roosevelt**

Not every fifteen-year-old can say they lived in a mansion. I can, but it, like so many other things in my journey, was a bit unusual.

You see, Coindre Hall in Huntington, Long Island, was indeed a mansion. It was built in 1912 in the style of a medieval French chateau and beautifully situated on several sprawling acres along the stunning shores of the Long Island Sound. It boasted 80,000 square feet with forty separate rooms. It was quite unique.

However, after being purchased by the Brothers of the Sacred Heart in 1964, it was converted into a Catholic boarding school for boys and functioned as such until

1971.

Although my experience at General Douglas MacArthur Military Academy in Mt. Freedom, New Jersey, was transformative in many ways, I so did not want to return for another year.

My sister, Roxie, lobbied on my behalf, and Dad agreed I could instead attend Coindre Hall. My new stepmother was Catholic, and her son had attended Coindre Hall. So, off to a Catholic boarding school I went in spite of the fact I had never even been inside of a Catholic Church.

Wearing a jacket and tie every day to class instead of the scratchy West Point Wannabe military uniform at Douglass MacArthur seemed quite liberating.

I, along with more than one hundred other eighth-graders, was awakened early every morning by the thunderous clapping of our prefect, Brother Arnold. The sound of Brother Arnold's clapping, which always signaled "stop talking and listen up," became even more familiar than the loud slapping sound of Brother Arnold's large Louisville Slugger-styled paddle going across a fellow student's butt.

Very early each morning, we gathered for prayer and devotions. These meetings always started with everyone reciting the Lord's Prayer and the Hail Mary prayer in unison. I knew the Lord's Prayer but had never in my life even heard the Catholic Hail Mary prayer.

Along with trying to fit in by stumbling through making the sign of the cross before we prayed, I really tried to pay close attention to this Hail Mary prayer.

Having never seen a printed version of the prayer, and with New Yorkers talking so fast anyway, I thought my new "family" was praying, "Hail Mary, blessed are thee and blessed is the fruit of the loom Jesus."

The mystery was solved after I saw a written version of the prayer and realized my fast-talking fellow students were saying, "...and blessed is the fruit of thy womb, Jesus!"

It was while I was attending Coindre Hall I learned I was "a Protestant." I had never heard that term before but soon learned I was the "only Protestant" in the entire school.

Once I learned to follow the rules and keep a listening ear for Brother Arnold's thunderclaps, life was good. After class, we could take off our jackets and tie, play sports, talk during meals, and even shoot some billiards in the recreation area.

All of our activities were highly structured. Whenever anyone deviated from the assigned activities or behavior, the spectacle of a fellow eighth-grader "assuming the position" in front of the student body and suffering three, four, or five *whacks* with a very large paddle was commonplace.

Usually, after three or four full-force *whacks*, the student would whimper or cry. The peer humiliation was the greater punishment. I managed to avoid Brother Arnold's paddle. I was fortunate to only get smacked once by Brother Arnold and was only kicked once by my math teacher, Mr. Sullivan (for having my leg too far in the aisle, away from my desk).

All of our teachers, except for Mr. Sullivan, were Brothers of the Sacred Heart. Most were excellent, engaging teachers. I thrived in this environment and made the honor roll every quarter. Along with math, English, history, and science, we had a full period of religion.

All of my classmates had attended several years of Catholic grade school and seemed quite bored and uninterested during religion class as Brother Joseph would discuss many of the teachings of the Catholic church.

This would include topics like the infallibility of the pope, confession to a priest, vows of poverty and chastity, praying to saints, the assumption of Mary, the belief that Mary was forever a virgin, and more.

This was all new to me, so my hand would often be the only one raised, usually with a question and not an answer.

At the end of each year, Coindre Hall had a grand commencement celebration with hundreds of family members coming from far and wide to retrieve their son after graduation.

During each commencement service, the principal awarded medals for scholastic excellence in each subject. As this grand celebration was approaching, I learned I was one of three finalists being considered to receive the science medal. I knew Dad was coming, and I was so hoping to win this award and make Dad proud. Dad was all about achievement and winning.

The big day came. All the students were seated on a large stage, and hundreds of family members seemed quite focused and interested as the ceremony unfolded. The big moment came as the scholastic medal winners were being called to stand at the front of the platform.

"This year, we are proud to present the science medal to a student who has demonstrated excellence throughout the year," the principal began. As soon as I learned the science medal was about to be presented, my heart was in my throat.

The principal continued, "And this year's science medal is awarded to Jim...Beatty."

It was as if this was happening in slow motion. As the principal was saying, Jim B.... I was preparing to stand, only to feel as if the rug had been pulled out from under me as he finished pronouncing Jim Beatty's last name.

I sat in silent disappointment feeling as if my favorite baseball team just lost the World Series. I was tuned out, and not half paying attention as the principal continued presenting the medals for scholastic excellence.

"This year's medal for scholastic excellence in the discipline of religion is presented to Jim Brissey," the principal announced. I really didn't even hear him. A student behind me pushed the back of my shoulder and said, "That's you. You won the religion medal."

As I went forward in a semi-shocked state, I heard

another student say. "They gave it to a blasted Protestant!"

Dad was proud and seemed to receive a vicarious thrill from the accolade.

Although I never joined the Catholic church, I did attend and graduate from a Catholic high school in Queens, New York, Msgr. McClancy Memorial High School.

There too, I was the only Protestant. In ways that I wasn't aware of at the time, God was preparing me for the work of the ministry, which would unfold many years later.

Now, as I look back fifty years, I can see God's handiwork with great joy. The old saying is so true, "hindsight is 20/20."

God works in ways we often do not see or understand at the time. Yet, His promise to "work all things together for our good" is very real.

As I have already shared, God's plan for my life has included serving on more than fifty *Via de Cristo* and *Kairos* interdenominational Christian renewal weekends.

One funny priceless memory I cherish involves a pastor friend named Don. Pastor Don wanted to serve on a *Kairos* prison weekend. In order to serve on the *Kairos* team, one must first attend a three-day *Via de Cristo* weekend and then attend eight to ten *Kairos* team meetings.

Pastor Don enjoyed his *Via de Cristo* weekend and gladly accepted an invitation to serve on a *Kairos* team. I picked Pastor Don up, and we drove together to his first *Kairos* team meeting. As we got in my car to go home after the meeting, Don looked ill. He was white as a ghost and had a sullen expression on his face.

"Don, are you okay?" I asked.

He responded by saying, "Jim, you didn't tell me."

"Didn't tell you what?" I inquired.

"You didn't tell me there would be a bunch of Catholics in the meeting."

I told Don, "I really didn't even think about it."

Then, in a tone conveying great surprise, he made a statement that hit me like the punch line of a good joke: "And they love Jesus!" LOL.

My friend, Pastor Don, had never met what I describe as "Christian Catholics." We had a good laugh about it on the way home and throughout our team meetings and *Kairos* weekend.

To this day, I tease my Catholic friends by saying, "Some of the best Catholics I know are Christians!"

The pearl of discovery is that we can customize that saying to fit any denomination. We can just as easily say, "Some of the best Baptists or Methodists or Lutherans are Christians!"

The point is, going to church doesn't make us a Christian any more than walking into McDonald's makes us a hamburger.

A recent Barna survey suggested more than 40 percent of regular church attenders have never had a born-again experience. I know firsthand how possible this may be.

You see, I almost missed heaven by eighteen inches, the distance from my head to my heart.

Oh, yes, as I was growing up, I knew in my mind what we were celebrating at Christmas and Easter. However, it was only after having my own personal road to Damascus encounter with Jesus on January 21, 1979, that I received Jesus in my heart.

I can so relate to what John Wesley said after his re-birth: "I felt my heart strangely warmed."

More than a half-century has passed since winning the religion medal at Coindre Hall. It has been more than forty years since I received Jesus in my heart and became born again.

My walk with Jesus has increasingly affirmed Christianity has nothing to do with intellectual ascent, religious pedigree, or the accolades of man. It has everything to do with having our hearts changed and set ablaze with the love of God.

In God's amazing grace, there is room for an illiterate plumber such as Smith Wigglesworth, a brilliant attorney like Charles Finney, a dairy farmer like Billy Graham, and even the likes of you and me!

# Faith Challenge Questions

- Have you ever felt like the oddball in a group?

- Have you ever worked hard to gain the approval of your mom or dad?

- Have you ever judged people based on their denomination or church membership?

- Have you had a born-again experience?

- What assures you that heaven is your home?

# *A Pearl of Love*

## Love Rolled Away the Stone

*"An angel of the Lord ...rolled back the stone"*
*(Matthew 28:2).*

Cast your lots for clothes you stripped
My beard is torn, My back is whipped
Put the nails deep in My bone
Love soon will roll away the stone
You are the branches, and I the vine
So keep your sponge of gall and wine
I'll take your sin as if My own
Love soon will roll away the stone
Take your spear and split My side
It is for you I'm crucified
My blood, your sins all did atone
Love soon will roll away the stone
So take My lifeless body down
Remove My thorny, bloodied crown
And place Me in My tomb alone
Love soon will roll away the stone
Let heaven and earth rejoice in Me
Love has triumphed through a cursed tree
Sound loud the trumpet, let all be shown

*My love has rolled away the stone*
*I have risen just as I said*
*The very firstborn from the dead*
*From this moment on, you're not alone*
*My love has rolled away the stone*
*Receive your new birth from above*
*As in the Jordan, a falling dove*
*Remember truth, a mustard seed sown*
*My love has rolled away the stone*
*Troubles and trials in this life are near*
*Be strong, take heart, be of good cheer*
*I sought you out; you are My own*
*My love has rolled away the stone*
*I will finish what I have begun*
*You are My workmanship and My son*
*Not one of you will I disown*
*My love has rolled away the stone*
*I have conquered all hell's damnation*
*I am the one and true foundation*
*Seated on my rightful throne*
*Soon love will bring My children home.*

# CHAPTER THIRTEEN:

# ACCOUNTABILITY OR PAIN?

*"If you don't know where you are going,*
*you'll end up someplace else."*
**Yogi Berra**

Have you ever been alone in a crowd? Lord knows I have.

Sure, I was alone in a crowd while attending military school and again when I was shipped off to Catholic boarding school. Yet, those experiences were nothing compared to the loneliness I felt during my three years at Brooklyn College.

There were more than 40,000 students enrolled in Brooklyn College while I attended, yet I have never felt more alone. I would never have darkened the doors of college if it wasn't for Mom. It was with great love and tremendous personal sacrifice my mom moved with me from North Carolina to Queens, New York, in 1972.

She did so to establish us as residents of New York, which made me eligible for the tuition-free City University of New York. This also made it possible for me to graduate high school from Msgr. McClancy, where I had attended my freshman and sophomore years.

My freshman and sophomore years at Msgr. McClancy were something out of a storybook. I made the honor roll each grading period, earned my freshman and varsity letters in track, and won the New York City Championships in high jump at the end of my sophomore year.

Binging home medals and trophies and scholastic awards pleased my dad. Looking back, I recognize that was the driving force of everything I was doing, "Gotta make Dad proud."

This all changed on August 13, 1971. That was the day I announced to Dad I would be leaving and moving to New Carolina to live with Mom and Roxie.

You see, Dad and Rosemarie had decided to move to Florida at the end of my sophomore year. If I had gone along with the move, I knew I would certainly not have the freedom to travel back to New York and visit my girlfriend.

As one might imagine, my announcement wasn't what Dad wanted to hear. Instead of going ballistic, as I imagined he might, Dad went silent. He didn't speak a word to me at all until the day I left for North Carolina. On the day I left, Rosemarie encouraged me to say goodbye to Dad before she drove me to the airport.

Dad was still in bed when I stuck my head into his bedroom and broke our silence. "I'm leaving now, Dad," I said with my heart in my throat.

"God bless you, Son," he said in somewhat of a muffled, heartbroken tone.

Those were the last words, the last communication of any form I had with my dad for the next seven years.

My "leaving dad" created a paradigm shift in my world. In one day, I went from being the all-American super-achieving son to becoming a Judas prodigal in his eyes.

The subsequent year at Fike H. S. in Wilson, North Carolina, was difficult. This southern public school had just recently integrated, and the racial tensions were palpable.

As I mentioned earlier, it was while attending Coindre Hall I discovered I was "a Protestant." Well, it was during my Junior year at Fike High School that I learned I was "a Yankee." This distinction of coming from north of the Mason-Dixon Line in 1971 was a much bigger deal to my classmates than most "Yankees" might imagine. One would think the Civil War had just ended. It seemed quite bizarre to me.

So, when Mom agreed that she and I could move back to New York where I could graduate from Msgr. McClancy and gain acceptance to the City University of New York; I was thrilled. I am and will forever be eternally grateful to my mom for making such a selfless sacrifice.

After graduating high school and getting enrolled in Brooklyn College, Mom moved back to North Carolina. I was, for the first time in my life, "alone."

Although there were more than 8 million fellow residents of New York at the time and, as I mentioned, more than 40,000 fellow students at Brooklyn College, I was alone in a crowd.

The first order of business after graduating Msgr. McClancy Memorial High School was to find a place to live. I found a room for rent in an old house in Kew Gardens, Queens.

It had a bed and a desk, and a small kitchenette equipped with a hot plate for a stove. The bathroom was out in the hall, but who cared about that? Certainly not me. Little did I know at the time this would be where my wife and I would celebrate our honeymoon and begin our life together in a few years!

I quickly realized I would need to work two or three jobs to afford to live on my own. So, my enthusiasm as a starry-eyed college student living on my own was soon dampened by an inhuman work and study schedule.

I enjoyed teaching karate at Tracy's Karate Studio in Forest Hills but dreaded my other job, driving a yellow cab in Manhattan. But, as my future father-in-law would often say, in his thick New York City accent, "You do what ya gotta do."

Allow me to pause from all this personal biographical sharing and ask you who are reading this to "stay with me." There is a valuable pearl of discovery coming which took me three years and a truckload of pain and disappointment to find.

So here I was, charging Hades with a squirt gun, chasing windmills of delusions, thinking I was going to work as hard as necessary to make grades good enough to gain acceptance into an optometric college. Proverbs 14:12 says, "There is way that appears right to be right, but in the end it leads to death."

I've never worked harder or been more disillusioned than I was for the next three years. I was "allowed" to see my girlfriend one day a week as she was consumed with becoming an orchestral conductor. My life consisted of teaching karate, driving a cab, and studying.

Carrying fifteen to seventeen credits per semester proved to be much more of a Herculean task than I had anticipated. Gone were the days of honor rolls and scholastic achievements. My best efforts were earning me a consistent C-plus average.

At the end of my junior year at Brooklyn College, I wrote the American Optometric Association and requested applications and information about the sixteen optometric colleges in the U. S. They sent me a great deal of information, including a listing of the qualifications of those students who had been accepted to their colleges over the past two years. The data was devastating. My grade point average wasn't even close to what I needed to apply.

The rude awakening that my last three years of hard work as a biology major at Brooklyn College were totally in vain was punctuated by breaking up with my girlfriend of six years.

As I look back, the next few months are a bit of a blur. No doubt my new crash diet of disappointment, pot, beer, and motorcycles played a major role in my diminished perspective. Gone was the all-American award-winning student-athlete.

My quest to somehow prove "I could make it without Dad's help" had failed. Like a ship without a rudder, I was lost and without direction. I had no plan B. Failure was not an option. Yet, becoming a college dropout with no prospects for the future was my new normal.

In the summer of my junior year at Brooklyn College, God did turn lemons into lemonade. On July 5, 1976, I met my bride, best friend, and lifelong ministry partner. However, that is not the pearl of discovery I want to share here.

The pearl I wish to share here is discovered as I look back at the loneliness, disillusionment, disappointment, and failure I endured during the three years I lived alone in my one-room "studio apartment."

It is perhaps best surmised by the slogan of the seminary I attended many years later, "without accountability, there is no responsibility."

"Accountability!" Now, *that* is a valuable pearl of wisdom. If we are not accountable to anyone for our choices, actions, and behaviors, we are an island unto ourselves and in serious jeopardy of making a mess of our life.

As I review the mess I made, I see God using the darkness of my pride and self-sufficiency like a master jeweler who rolls out the black velvet before rolling out the beautiful pearl.

But, what if someone younger than me, and Lord knows there seems to be more and more of such persons around me, could learn from my mistakes and poor choices. Looking at my past mistakes, I see my most grievous errors were not things I did. Rather, they were things I didn't do and should have done!

In my case, if I had sought some counsel about the requirements of becoming an optometrist while I was still in high school, I could have avoided three years of laboring in vain.

In *Via de Cristo*, we say, "An isolated Christian is a paralyzed Christian." To discover we are not created or designed to live our life as a Lone Ranger, doing what we want, when we want, how we want, is truly a pearl of great value.

In Ecclesiastes 4:9–10, Solomon, the wisest man who ever lived, said, "Two are better than one …If either of them falls down, one can help the other up."

Jesus had his good reasons for sending out His disciples two by two. Yes, a three-chord strand is not easily broken (Ecclesiastes 4:12). Why, even Jesus, the very Son of

God, needed help carrying His cross. Who are we to think
we don't need any help carrying ours?

# Faith Challenge Questions

- Have you ever felt alone in a crowd?

- Who do you hold yourself accountable to?

- When in your life did you experience
  disappointment?

- How have you responded to unexpected
  disappointment?

- Has suffering disappointment made you bitter or
  better?

# CHAPTER FOURTEEN:

# LIFE AND DEATH

*"He is no fool who gives up what he cannot keep to gain that which he cannot lose."*

**Jim Elliot**

Scripture tells us in Revelation 12:11, "They triumphed over him by the blood of the Lamb and by the word of their testimony." I like to say, "A person with a testimony is never at the mercy of a person with an argument."

Remember the blind man Jesus healed in the eighth chapter of the Gospel of John? He overcame the hateful diatribe of the Pharisees and Sadducees and wouldn't-sees and couldn't-sees who were offended by his healing. He did so by simply stating the obvious; "One thing I do know. I was blind but now I see!" (John 9:25). *Boom!* Drop the mic! Case dismissed.

Psalm 145:4 says, "One generation commends your

works to another." As we share with each other the wonderful things the Lord has done, God is glorified, and we are strengthened in our faith. This is precisely what I am endeavoring to do with this book, glorify God and strengthen you.

When we share testimonies of what God has done, we glorify God, shut the devil's mouth, and strengthen one another's faith. I believe this is why Hebrews chapter 11 is often referred to as "the faith chapter." In Hebrews 11, we are encouraged by many people who, through different circumstances, discovered God's goodness and faithfulness.

In Romans 1:11–12, Paul says, "I long to see you so that I may impart to you some spiritual gift to make you strong— that is, that you and I may be mutually encouraged by each other's faith."

This is the heartbeat of four of the sixty-seven classes in our Higher Ground School of Ministry, which we refer to as: "Great Men & Women of Faith."

I shared in the opening of the book how HGSM was born. The four classes I am referring to focus on twelve great men and women of faith. In these classes, we share the testimonies of a variety of different ordinary people who were used in extraordinary ways by our awesome God.

Our faith is supercharged by looking into the lives of people including Billy Graham, Mother Teresa, Charles Finney, Smith Wigglesworth, Kathryn Kuhlman, David

Livingstone, John Wesley, Francis Asbury, and more.

When we go beyond the historical and biographical sketches of such individuals and enter the genuine spiritual ramifications of such God encounters, we discover a life-changing, attitude-rearranging pearl. Namely, if our awesome God uses ordinary people in extraordinary ways, then He can use you and me!

Before diminishing or disqualifying the testimonies of the above-mentioned individuals on the basis that they are no longer living, remember the authors of Scripture are also among the faithful departed. The glorious Gospels of Matthew, Mark, Luke, and John are prime examples of testimonies from faithful men. The testimonies of the faithful become "faith fuel" when we embrace them.

As I mentioned earlier, Paul exhorts us by reminding us that "we may have ten thousand counselors, but few fathers in the faith." For even the best counsel to have a positive impact, one must be tuned in with a listening ear. Ancient Chinese Tao Te Ching philosophy hits the bullseye with its saying: "When the student is ready, the teacher appears."

I pray the Holy Spirit gives you "ears to hear" what He wants you to as I share a couple of testimonies that enlarged my faith. I pray they will enlarge and strengthen your faith as well.

Prison ministry was the last thing I thought I would be involved in. I certainly never dreamed I would be on death row in Raiford, Florida. Yet, after many years of prison ministry, which included outreaches to a dozen state prisons in Florida, one in North Carolina, and two in Honduras, an uninvited nudge from the Lord began compelling me to reach out to the 330 men on Florida's death row.

I met with the chaplain at Union Correctional. This old prison was, at one time, known as "The Rock," the home of Florida's infamous electric chair, Old Sparky, and was the prison popularized in the movie, *The Green Mile*, with actor Tom Hanks.

The chaplain graciously tried to talk me out of "going on the row." He shared how, when he first began his work as a chaplain, he spent five years trying to reach the inmates on the row for Christ without one convert. After listening to this good man's suggestions for reaching out to other areas within the prison, I told him, "I just have one problem."

"What problem is that?" he asked.

"I believe the Holy Spirit is leading me to reach out with the gospel to the men on the row."

With the chaplain's reluctant but sincere blessing, he walked me down several areas on death row. The sign above this area of the prison says, "Condemned Row." The atmosphere and spiritual climate in this "prison within the prison" lives up to that billing.

Death row in Raiford is a large two-story building with dozens of individual rows of cells housing more than 300 men. Each row has about fifteen cells, approximately six by eight feet in size. Each jail cell faces a drab gray wall. There are no windows. It is cold in the winter and hot in the summer. The men remain in their cells twenty-three hours a day. The spiritual oppression on the row is so palpable it hangs in the air like a thick unwelcome fog.

One of the first sobering realities I noticed on the row, as the chaplain spoke to a few of the inmates, was none of the inmates he spoke to even knew who he was. The row is a very lonely, isolated, and depressing place.

After my brief orientation, I was on my own. As I meandered down each of the condemned rows, I walked very slowly, trying to read the body language of each man.

Although it was early in the afternoon, most of the men lay comatose in bed. If I were to put a sign over most of the cells to describe what I discovered, it would read something like, "Throw dirt on me; I'm already dead."

Occasionally, an inmate would acknowledge my uninvited presence by making brief eye contact and then quickly glance away, signaling their disinterest in having their depressed, isolated condition disturbed.

Then there was Manny. Here's an excerpt from my book, *A Shepherd's Heart*:

# Manny's Story

*My good friend, Manny Valle*

Manny Valle was a rambunctious twenty-seven-year-old kid who made one very bad decision: a decision that cost him his life. During a routine traffic stop in Coral Gables, Florida, over thirty years ago, Manny panicked and shot a police officer. Officer Pena died. Manny spent the next thirty-three years in a six-by-nine-foot cell on death row in Starke, Florida. He was allowed out of his cell for one hour, two times per week.

Four years ago, as we were sharing the gospel from cell to cell on death row, God blessed me and my friend "Gator" with the amazing honor of leading Manny to Christ. It was the "real deal."

When we first met Manny, we talked about anything

except Jesus. We talked about Philly steak sandwiches, the Philadelphia Phillies, the New York Jets, Mustang automobiles, and more. At that time, Manny had been on death row for twenty-nine years, and he didn't know Jesus from a can of paint.

God's love was present in a strong way, even as we simply talked about this and that. It was like watching a snowball melt in a microwave as Manny began to realize we weren't there to beat him up with a Bible. It must have been thirty or forty minutes into our conversation before Gator and I began to share our testimonies and explain the difference between "religion" and a relationship with Jesus.

Before we knew it, Manny had one hand raised through the bars holding my hand and the other holding Gator's. Tears ran down his face as we led him in the sinner's prayer, and Manny Valle gave his heart to Jesus. The very first question I asked Manny after he said, "Amen," was, "Manny, do you have a Bible?" He said no. At that very second, a volunteer opened the door about sixty feet away and yelled down the row, "Anybody needs a Bible?"

The three of us laughed and cried at the same time, "Yes! Right here!" Gator and I signed Manny's Bible, said so long, and went on our way.

Manny became a close friend with Jesus that day. And he soon became a dear friend of mine. I drove up to Starke every few months to surprise Manny with a visit: but I was always the one who left death row renewed and revived! What a difference Jesus makes! With every letter and every visit, I marveled at Manny's humble and grateful heart. Like a bright light in a dark place, Manny's faith and sense of humor changed the atmosphere. He was a Christian. He was a friend.

God blessed me with a wonderful three-hour visit with Manny while he was on death watch, just a few days before he was executed. We laughed more than anything else. Manny was beautifully clothed in the peace that passes all human understanding. Before I said goodbye, he looked me in the eye and said, "Jim, I will meet you at the Pearly Gates with a Philly steak sandwich and a box of cannoli! And give my love to Jean."

Manny was executed at Florida State Prison on September 28, 2011, at 7:04 p.m. They offered him a tranquilizer before escorting him to the death chamber. He refused. Manny died in peace. He died in Christ. We prayed and cried with his family in Starke during his execution. I miss him. Yet, whenever I am feeling blue, I think of Manny's big smile, and my world is a bit brighter.

> Each year, for seven years, on the anniversary of Manny's death, we paid a special visit to each one of the rows. Sometimes it was Gator and me. Sometimes our friend, Bobby, would join us. On one such occasion, I flew solo.
>
> We followed the protocol I felt the Lord gave us on each row every time. The guard would give us access to the row with a loud buzzing noise. We then opened the very heavy metal door and stepped onto the row. The loud clanging of the door slamming behind us

would send a loud and clear signal to the men on that row that someone was there.

Whatever small talk that may have been going on among those prisoners who were awake, would quickly halt out of curiosity, while several inmates would hold a mirror out of their cell to investigate the intruders.

In a loud voice, amplified by the cold cinderblock walls, I announced, "On September 28, 2011, the state of Florida executed our friend, Manny Valle. We came here today to give you this gift in his honor."

Then we would sing Amazing Grace. As soon as we finished singing, I would raise my voice and say, "Manny Valle died with courage. Manny died with dignity. Manny died in faith. Before Manny died, he received Jesus as his personal Savior. If you would like to pray and invite Jesus to be your Savior, please let us know as we walk by."

We then walked very slowly down the row, sometimes with complete silence. On some rows, men would whisper, "Thank You," as we walked by. On some rows men would stand grasping the bars on their cell waiting to pray. On every anniversary, more than a dozen of the more than 300 men on Condemned Row prayed with us and committed their life to Jesus.

For more than fifteen of the thirty-three years Manny lived on The Row, his friend, Lucky, lived in the cell next to him. Ironically, the only two men I have ever known named, "Lucky" lived on Death Row.

# Faith Challenge Questions

- When was the last time you sang "Amazing Grace"?

- When was the first time you sang "Amazing Grace"?

- Do you know who wrote "Amazing Grace" and under what circumstances?

- How has God's amazing grace touched and changed your life?

# A Pearl of Victory

## A Candle Burned

*"Let your light shine" (Matthew 5:16)*

*A candle burned*
*On the cold, dark row*
*A graceful fire*
*A warm Christ-glow*

*A bit colder now*
*A bit darker still*
*The cold dark row*
*The cold dark row.*

# CHAPTER FIFTEEN:

# GRACE FOR THE HUMBLE

*"True humility is not thinking less of yourself;*
*it is thinking of yourself less."*

**C. S. Lewis**

Much of Jesus' earthly ministry involved Him teaching in simple stories known as parables. If we are listening, we can learn a lot from such stories.

As mentioned earlier, the apostle Paul tells us, "We may have ten thousand counselors." It's fair to say that we are created to learn from others, however young or old, big or small. We can glean wisdom by observing the habits and practices of successful people. We can also receive a sober warning by recognizing the mistakes and pitfalls of the fallen.

In the previous chapter, I shared about my friend, Manny. During the last four years of the thirty-three years he spent on death row, he truly did become a good friend and a great inspiration to me. Yet, his life and execution serve as a vivid reminder of what can happen when bad choices are made.

When Manny was a twenty-something "kid" in South Florida, he and his friends panicked after being stopped for a traffic violation in a stolen car. Manny shot two police officers. One of the officers died, and Manny paid the ultimate price for his crime.

It was discovered later that the computer in the officer's patrol car wasn't working at the time. The police officers had no way of learning the car was stolen. The entire incident could have been avoided. No doubt those involved and their families paid a great price for one young, panicked man's terrible choice.

As I press on in sharing some of the "pearls" I have discovered along the way, serving as a shepherd for twenty-five years, there is one pearl many never find. I'm referring to the very valuable pearl of humility. James wasn't kidding when he said, "God opposes the proud but shows favor to the humble" (James 4:6).

As a newly married man, more than forty years ago, I made a very silly split-second decision which serves as a good, yet somewhat painful, illustration of how "pride goes before a fall" (Proverbs 16:18).

Because my wife and I were expecting a baby when we got married, our marriage was viewed as being quite scandalous by Jean's grandparents, all of whom were old-fashioned Italian immigrants. So, when Jean's grandmother gave us a wedding gift in the form of a $1,000 money order made out to "Jean Dattoma" (Jean's maiden name was Dattoma), I pridefully and foolishly tore the money order up into little pieces and mailed it back to my new grandmother-in-law with a note saying, "Jean's name is Jean Brissey, not Jean Dattoma."

How dumb can you be and still breathe? I really showed her, didn't I? At the time, Jean and I didn't have two pennies to rub together. The simple truth is sin will make you stupid.

I know of no sin that is sneakier and more destructive than pride. Pride is like bad breath. You don't know you have it, but everyone around you suffers from it. It is something we all fall to from time to time in various ways. As a matter of fact, if we think we have achieved humility, we just lost it!

Many go through life as their own worst enemy with the unholy trinity of "me, myself, and I" on the throne of their constant despair and calamity. However, some fortunate folks do come to discover the breakthrough power of humility.

One such individual is a thirty-one-year-old husband and father in our church by the name of Malachi. Malachi came to our church when he was just seventeen years old. We actually had an intervention for him as his life was spinning out of control at the time.

Malachi received the love and care that was poured out

to him during our group expression of tough love. He got on track with the Lord, fell in love, got married, became a dad, and had a good job as a general manager and personal trainer at a large upscale health spa.

Malachi had some fresh ideas about starting his own business. However, when he would share these ideas with the members of the spa, the owner would get very upset. The owner got so upset by this that, one day, he went into a rage and fired Malachi right on the spot. Malachi called me and asked for my counsel as he was walking to his car. I explained to Malachi that the answer to his question about what he should do was "simple but not easy."

Even now, as I look back upon the humility exercised that day by the then twenty-four-year-old Malachi, I marvel.

I shared with Malachi that he should turn around and walk right back into the spa where he had just been summarily fired and apologize to the owner. I encouraged Malachi that if he did that, one of two things would happen. He might get his job back, but even if he didn't, he would always have the satisfaction of knowing that he did everything he could to leave the job in a good way.

Malachi received my advice like a champ and did exactly as I (his pastor & mentor) suggested. He didn't get his job back, but the red-faced irate owner did calm down, and Malachi left the job with dignity and humility.

It seemed like only a few weeks after this fierce demonstration of humility, Malachi's new business began to take off and prosper.

Along with completing Higher Ground School of Ministry Track I & II and serving as an ordained evangelist, Malachi and his wife and ministry partner, Angel, have prospered. They now have two beautiful, healthy boys and three or four thriving businesses.

About a year ago, as Malachi and I were having lunch, he shared with me how he was believing for a Lamborghini. As we were walking away from the restaurant, a Lamborghini unexpectedly pulled up to the traffic light. We have lived in DeLand for more than twenty years. I had never seen a Lamborghini in DeLand until that very day.

A couple of months ago, Malachi pulled into the church parking lot with a beautiful white ($260,000) Lamborghini convertible. Did I mention he paid cash for it?

*Malachi and his paid for Lamborghini*

A couple of weeks ago, while his paid-for Lambo was home in his driveway, young Malachi drove into church in a ($260,000) Bentley. Yes, he paid cash for the Bentley as well.

No matter how much success Malachi and Angel enjoy moving forward, I will always remember receiving that desperate phone call from the freshly fired twenty-four-year-old Malachi and witnessing such a powerful display of genuine humility. Yes! God gives grace to the humble but opposes the proud!

Humility is a lot like pearls in that it can be authentic or fake. False humility can be even more sneaky than pride. A good example of false humility is when someone tells the preacher, "Good sermon, Pastor," and they respond by saying. "Oh, it's not me, it's the Lord" or "It's all God."

Well, if it was "all God," you wouldn't be here!

A truly humble response to someone saying, "Good sermon, Pastor," would be a simple "thank you."

There is no greater example of true humility than Jesus. Paul tells us in Philippians 2 that Jesus, though being in very nature God, humbled Himself and took on the very nature of a servant. Humility and servanthood go hand in glove.

We recently were blessed to witness another inspiring example of authentic humility, also demonstrated by a graduate of Higher Ground School of Ministry (I better guard my heart against pride as I share about another HGSM grad!)

Darren and Rose are truly one of the most gracious Jesus-loving couples we have ever met. They have served in many forms of Christian outreach throughout the Tampa area for decades. Their dream was to someday be employed and serve as part of a pastoral staff with a church. When they discovered Higher Ground School of Ministry offered an affordable path to earn fully accredited ministry credentials online at their own pace, Darren was all in.

Darren took to HGSM like a duck to water. Most ministry students complete the sixty-seven-class curriculum in about fourteen to eighteen months. Darren completed HGSM Track I in about nine months and immediately tackled HGSM Track II. He also completed HGSM Track II in about nine months and received full Ordination.

Soon after his Ordination, I received a phone call from Darren, asking me if I would send a recommendation letter to a church in Tampa where he was applying for a position as associate pastor. Of course, I was happy to oblige.

I was floored when Darren gave me the information about who I should send the letter to. As it turned out, the point person was someone who had served as associate pastor at a church in Tampa where Jean and I served as children's ministers. We had not seen or heard from Pastor George in thirty-five years!

Darren and Rose were like kids at Christmas as Darren was hired on staff as associate pastor at this large, very well-established church in Tampa. Pastor Darren and

Rose served the senior pastor and church members with great diligence and excellence. It was a thing of beauty to behold.

After more than a year of serving at this church with all their heart, I received a phone call from Pastor Darren saying he had abruptly resigned. I was floored again, but this time, not in a good way. I knew how elated Darren and Rose were to finally be employed as a part of a pastoral staff of a very respected established church. This news was hard to digest.

It turned out that a woman in the church had made false accusations against Darren. He was so appalled by the false accusations and what he perceived as the lackluster response from administration that he got offended and submitted his resignation.

As we talked about what had happened, it became clear that Darren, in his upset state, had overreacted. My counsel to Darren was similar to the counsel I gave Malachi many years before. I recommended that Darren go back to the senior pastor and ask for his forgiveness for overreacting and ask for his job back.

Darren did exactly what I suggested. However, the senior pastor responded by saying Darren couldn't have his job back because he had already announced to their large congregation that Pastor Darren had resigned.

Darren called me right after his request to be reinstated as associate pastor was denied. I recommended Darren go back to the senior pastor again and ask for his blessing for him and Rose to continue serving in the church. In addition, ask the senior pastor if, whenever the Lord would lead, at a future time of the senior pastor's choosing, he might prayerfully consider reinstating Darren as associate pastor.

The senior pastor agreed, and within a few short months, Pastor Darren was reinstated as full-time associate pastor.

Truly, God gives grace to the humble.

In his book, *The Touch of God*, Dr. Rodney Howard-Browne says, "Humility is the clothing of the Spirit. It lays its life down in order to lift others up."

We have never known anyone who has walked in a more dynamic humility than the Rev. Billy Graham. After meeting him and spending time with him, my wife and I both describe Mr. Graham as a "humble general."

Immediately after his final evangelistic crusade in flushing Meadow, New York, Billy Graham was asked by a reporter to comment on his amazing ministry career. His response was classic Billy Graham. Rev. Graham said, "If you are walking through the woods and you see a turtle sitting atop a fence post, would you conclude the turtle got there on his own or did someone put him there?" *Boom!* Drop the mic!

We do our best, and God will take care of the rest.

# Faith Challenge Questions

- Looking back, when has foolish pride tripped you up?

- Who do you have in your life to ask questions of?

- How has God given you favor in your work?

- What are you believing God for?

# A Pearl of Deliverance

## The Cross

*"May I never boast except in the cross"*
*(Galatians 6:14).*

*The cross is stained red*
*With the blood that was shed*
*On a tree*
*On dark Calvary;*
*The darkness and pain,*
*Disgrace and the shame,*
*Made clear for the world*
*To see:*
*With a crown of sharp thorns,*
*Crowds of insults and scorns,*
*He willingly bled there*
*For me.*
*Oh, grave, where is your victory?*
*Oh, death, where is your sting?*
*The enemy is defeated!*
*"Jesus!" is the song I sing.*
*Sing aloud the cry of victory!*
*Let all the world behold*
*The beauty of an empty cross*

*And so the story's told*
*Of a fisher of men from Nazareth*
*And the Sea of Galilee,*
*Who caught me in His net of love*
*And set my spirit free.*
*His name, above every other,*
*Should be high and lifted up;*
*Lift high the name of Jesus*
*And He'll overflow your cup.*
*His love and joy and peace*
*And patience and kindness too,*
*Are fruit of His Holy Spirit,*
*Given for me and you.*
*Seek the fullness of His Spirit*
*While He can yet be found,*
*For where the Holy Spirit is*
*Truth and freedom will abound.*
*So on Resurrection Sunday*
*May your hope be raised anew,*
*In the blessed name of Jesus:*
*The King of all the Jews.*

## CHAPTER SIXTEEN:

# A FIREHOUSE REVISITED

*"Explore. Dream. Discover."*

**Mark Twain**

"You can't take a forty-year-old head and stick it on twenty-year-old shoulders."

This pearl of wisdom was shared with me by my New York City firefighter father-in-law, Joe; God rest his soul.

It's funny, but so many of Joe's colorful sayings seem to become more and more true as time passes. Of course, they don't become truer. It is our perspective that changes over time.

Although Joe has been in heaven for more than a decade, I can often hear his big loud voice echoing in my mind: "Do da right ting," he would often say.

"Don't believe anything you hear and half of what you see," was another one of Joe's gems.

We know God is the judge, and we are convinced we will see Joe in heaven, but Joe was no teetotaling churchgoer. He was big and loud and often abrasive. Yet, he would run into a burning building for a stranger. That's what he did for a living in Queens, New York, for twenty-two years.

I picked Joe up from his firehouse in Woodhaven on the day he was injured while fighting a fire. He had lost a lot of blood after his arm was severely lacerated by a falling piece of glass. Joe was white as a sheet and uncharacteristically quiet during the ride home.

That was the last fire Joe ever fought, but he never quit being a fighter. He fought long and hard against the city of New York and won his settlement for three-quarter pay for the rest of his life.

Twenty years later, Joe fought long and hard in his battle against cancer. In all my years of ministry, I have never seen any individual withstand the rigors and side effects of chemotherapy like Joe. For the first three years of his seven-year battle, Joe endured the treatments like a champ.

Slowly, however, cancer and the chemo wore Big Joe down, and after a brief stint in Hospice, Joe passed. I was honored to hold his hand when he died. I felt an angel lift his spirit out of his body. I'm confident we will see Joe again.

One of the pearls we have discovered during our twenty-five-plus years of outreach ministry is the importance of being "pre-prayered." Whether you are walking into a cancer treatment center, a prison, or a mission field, it is critical to spend time in prayer before you take your first step.

Several years ago, just a few years after Joe passed, Jean and I felt prompted by the Holy Spirit to lead a mission trip to the streets of New York. Many of our Florida church members had never been to New York and signed on for the adventure right away.

Before bringing the team of about a dozen outreach ministers to hit the streets of the Big Apple, Jean and I went to New York to "pre-prayer." New York is a big city, and we sincerely wanted God's direction as to where the Lord would have our team go.

We had a splendid trip. Snow was still falling as our plane landed at New York's LaGuardia Airport. The entire city was covered with a fresh blanket of snow. It was beautiful. Everything looked unusually fresh and clean. The garbage cans were topped with three to four inches of new snow. They looked like giant ice cream cones as our taxi carried us to Astoria.

Our trip was blessed from start to finish. Before we unpacked our suitcases, we enjoyed a long chilly walk in Astoria Park. It was fun seeing the big park empty and dressed in snow white. Icicles hung playfully from the trees, reflecting the bright lights from the Triborough Bridge in a playful way.

We took many long walks over the next few days. We walked all over Queens. Sometimes to enjoy a new restaurant, but always with a questioning heart as to where the Lord would have us bring the team in just a few weeks.

One of the most important truths we have discovered in our journey is the difference between a "good idea" and a "God idea." They are often two very different things.

Bringing a mission team to hit the streets of New York City was a "God idea," and we "knew in our knowers" the importance of "going where the Lord said, 'Go'" and "doing what the Lord said, 'Do.'" As I mentioned, this is where we discover what I call "the sweet spot of God's grace."

When we "go where the Lord says, 'Go,'" and do what the Lord says, 'Do,'" there is a supernatural peace that comes. This special grace was upon Jean and me as we walked and "pre-prayed" for our outreach to the streets of New York.

*N.Y.C. Mission Team at Engine 325, Woodhaven, Queens*

We ventured by my late father-in-law's firehouse in Woodhaven, Queens, with a question in our hearts. Could this be one of the places the Holy Spirit would have us bring our mission team? Minutes after knocking on the big metal firehouse door, a surprisingly friendly soul greeted us with a great big smile. He was the lieutenant in charge of the firehouse. We introduced ourselves and explained our plan to bring a team from Florida to share the gospel on the streets of New York.

When Jean shared how her dad had been a firefighter at this very firehouse, our new lieutenant friend became even more curious. He had heard of Joe but had never met him.

When we asked if we could bring our mission team by and make lunch for the firefighters, his response was classic. With a very thick New York accent, our lieutenant said, "You's guys come, and we will cook you's lunch!"

In an almost comical and transparent way, he went on to say, "But listen, my guys ain't really church-going guys, so don't be offended if day don't want to hear no preaching."

We shared a good laugh and then explained how those were the very people we were hoping to talk to during our mission outreach. We shared contact information, and I promised to let him know when we planned to come by.

There were some other parks and neighborhoods we felt the Lord was highlighting, but we knew right away that our outreach to the firehouse was going to be special.

Weeks later, our team of about a dozen outreach ministers landed in New York. It's cold in New York in the wintertime, but the New York City chill didn't quench the Holy Spirit fire burning in the hearts of our precious team members.

We found our lieutenant friend to be true to his word. He and his firefighters made ten of us a ravioli dinner that couldn't have been more delicious. As enjoyable as the food was, the entertainment we received was even better. The lieutenant was also spot on in saying his firefighters weren't church people. They were obviously leery about us, Jesus people, and kept their distance. Yet, the comradery of the men at the firehouse was palpable and each of the seven firefighters working that shift seemed to have a great sense of humor.

The lieutenant tried to break the ice by saying, "Listen, da firefighter dats about to come in is very handsome. He's so handsome, we call him 'Face.' So, when he comes in, if all you ladies can say, 'Ooooh, look how handsome he is,' we can make him blush."

With unbridled hilarity, that's exactly what happened next. The ladies did just as instructed, and in perfect unison, all said, "Ooooh, look how handsome he is." The firefighter blushed, and then we all cracked up laughing as he slowly realized how the lieutenant had set him up.

As Yogi Berra once said, "Like *déjà vu* all over again," this scenario soon repeated itself as the lieutenant said, "Now dis next guy dats gonna come in is very strong and has big muscles. So, when he comes in, if all you ladies can say, 'Ooooh, look how big his muscles are,' we can embarrass him." As if it had been rehearsed, the ladies on our team obliged and with the same truly hilarious result.

Although we all shared a couple of good laughs and our lieutenant friend couldn't have been more hospitable, the other firefighters were noticeably standoffish and kept their distance as our team noshed on the scrumptiously prepared meal of ravioli and hot Italian bread.

As only the Lord could have orchestrated, the lieutenant ended up sitting directly across from our team member, Michelle, who had been a New York City police officer and was also a 9/11 miracle survivor. We soon discovered our jovial life-loving lieutenant friend was also a 9/11 survivor. As the two began to swap stories about their experiences when the Twin Towers fell, the other firefighters, with uncharacteristic timidity, slowly drew closer to the conversation. Before long, they were all circled around our dinner table, listening to these heroic accounts.

It soon became clear the Lord was rolling out the red carpet for us to present the gospel. The atmosphere in the room had shifted from loud laughter and multiple simultaneous conversations to one of great solemnity as we all listened intently to heart-touching 9/11 testimonies.

When the time was right, I lifted my voice and addressed all in the room. I explained, "We weren't religious; we just loved Jesus and that it was Jesus who called us to come from Florida to tell them God loved them and wanted a relationship with each one of them."

When given the opportunity to pray, every one of these brave men bowed their heads with great humility and sincerity. When we gave the invitation for anyone to receive Jesus into their heart for the first time, one firefighter lifted his hand, and we all prayed the sinner's prayer. It was a Holy and unforgettable moment.

Many souls were saved during that mission trip. The team served with love, sacrifice, and excellence. Like when they went to Central Park on their "day off" to buy a dirty water dog (New York City hot dog) only to give all their money to a homeless pregnant teen. They left Central Park that day with their stomachs empty but their hearts full as the young woman had received Jesus as her Savior.

Of all the God-blessed encounters we had during that outreach, the one firefighter lifting his hand and receiving Jesus stands out to me. Perhaps "that" is the pearl of discovery I am trying to point to in all my rambling about this one outreach: "It's about the one!"

Praise God for Billy Graham and all those gifted and called to mass crusade evangelism. Jesus also touched thousands in a single meeting at times, as He did with His sermon on the Mount. Peter touched thousands with one sermon on Pentecost, and the apostle Paul often raised his voice to address a large crowd. Praise God for such magnificent demonstrations and mass gatherings.

However, we must never forget the importance of reaching out to the one. We must remember how Jesus reached out to one thirsty soul when He encountered the woman at the well or how He stunned the crowd when He called Zacchaeus down from the Sycamore tree. Amidst all the hullabaloo of a loud excited crowd, Jesus singled out blind Bartimaeus. He responded to and commended the faith of the Roman Centurion, the woman with the issue of blood, and the woman with her alabaster box. Jesus went so far as to exhort the foot-washing alabaster box-breaking woman by declaring that her one sacrificial act of love would be shared wherever the gospel was to be preached!

Jesus purposefully made a holy spectacle of one dead man named Lazarus. He stopped an entire funeral procession to raise one dead boy and bless the widow at Nain. In Acts chapter 8, we read how Philip was translated to reach the one Ethiopian eunuch. In Acts 16, we witness a most courageous and supernatural act of compassion as Paul and Silas reach out to save one suicidal jailer.

Perhaps the greatest example of reaching out to the one took place during Jesus' last hours on earth as He reached out from the cross to one lost sinner dying next to Him. One of the last declarations Jesus made while on earth was to one common crucified thief, as He promised, "Today you will be with me in paradise" (Luke 23:43).

Praise God for worldwide telecasts, mass crusades, and mega-churches that reach tens of thousands. God is the righteous judge, and He will ultimately sift the wheat from the tares. Yet, in His parable of the Pearl of Great Price, we see the heart of God beating for the one.

Jesus, the Good Shepherd, is always willing to "leave the ninety-nine to find the one lost sheep." How am I so sure? I know it is so because He came and rescued me.

# Faith Challenge Questions

- How has your outlook on life changed in the last ten or twenty years?

- Can you share a time you had a close moment with Christ?

- When was the last time you laughed so hard you teared up or had your belly hurt?

- Can you name one person who greatly impacted your life?

- What was it about that person that impacted you so?

# *A Pearl of Life*

## Mary's Marvel

*"Mary treasured up all these things ...in her heart"*
*(Luke 2:19).*

*How Mary must have marveled*
*That very first Christmas Eve:*
*Not by power nor by might,*
*But by His Spirit—just believe!*
*Shrouded by the quiet*
*Amidst the hay and straw,*
*Joseph and the shepherds*
*Bow down in reverent awe.*
*The Lord of all creation,*
*Who made the Sabbath rest,*
*Decided to Himself come down*
*And lie at Mary's breast.*
*The glory-filled small manger*
*Must have caused the stars to dim;*
*The promise of the ages,*
*Now all fulfilled in Him.*
*In joyful, holy splendor*
*They journeyed from afar:*
*Three kings, three gifts, three Persons*

*One bright and Morning Star.*
*Gold they brought for kingship:*
*He is the King of kings,*
*The Alpha, the Omega,*
*Of whom all creation sings.*
*Incense they brought for priesthood:*
*Our intercessor, our high priest;*
*To become the very greatest,*
*One must first become the least.*
*Myrrh was brought for burial: Our blameless*
*sacrifice.*
*This is chiefly why He came. Nothing less would*
*suffice.*
*Not by His birth He saved us nor to live on earth He*
*came, but to give His life a ransom, Lost sinners to*
*reclaim.*
*At the foot of an ugly cross*
*Stared a mother at her son,*
*As she questioned why she heard*
*"It is finished; it is done!"*
*How Mary must have marveled*
*That very first Easter morn:*
*"Why seek the living among the dead?*
*Woman, this is why I was born."*
*I came to give life to My bride*
*For I am that I am the Bridegroom;*
*So hearts would be full like the manger*
*Not cold like the empty tomb!*

# CHAPTER SEVENTEEN:

# A BAD QUESTION

*"I always pray for God's guidance in my life, and
He always provides it."*

**Dr. Ben Carson**

There is always higher ground in God. That's a fact.
Reminding ourselves of this often can save us from
stalling in our spiritual growth or, worse yet, backsliding
in our faith.

In 1 Corinthians 10:12, Paul cautions us by saying,
"So, if you think you think you are standing firm, be
careful that you don't fall." Yet, in Philippians 4:6, the
same apostle Paul exhorts us to "not be anxious [careful]
about anything." So, which is it? I believe the answer is,
"Yes." This may be bad grammar, but it's good theology.
Let me explain.

When it comes to thinking too much of ourselves or

slipping into taking God's grace and presence for granted, we better be careful. The older we get, the more readily we can recount called men and women who were once on fire for God but grew cold to the things of God. Disappointment, disillusionment, and offense have sidelined many in the body of Christ.

John Wesley's concern for the church he founded is truer today than ever. Wesley said,

> *My fear is not that our great movement, known as the Methodists, will eventually cease to exist or one day die from the earth. My fear is that our people will become content to live without the fire, the power, the excitement, the supernatural element that makes us great.*

When it comes to becoming cold or complacent to the things of God, we certainly should be careful. Our journey with Jesus is a marathon, not a sprint. How we finish our race is more important than how we start. Will we hear those words, "Well done" from our Savior, or will He say, "Well, it's done"?

However, when it comes to reaching out to the lost, there is no benefit in being too careful. No, in such endeavors, we should be careful about nothing. Our presentation of the gospel doesn't have to be pristine in order to be effective. If our authentic testimony is backed up with a genuine love walk with Jesus, it will have an impact.

If we are to finish our race well, it will be because of the grace and unmerited favor of God. However, we must continue to "do our best and trust God to do the rest!"

I love that Philippians 2:12 and Philippians 2:13 don't have a period separating them. In Philippians 2:12, Paul exhorts us to "work out [our] salvation with fear and trembling." In the same breath, Paul goes on in the very next verse to remind us, "it is God who is working in you to will and to act according to His good pleasure."

When we add 1 Corinthians 6:17 to the discussion, this conundrum becomes clearer. "Whoever is united with the Lord is one with him in spirit." So, we are dust fused to glory! We continue to have free will, yet we are not alone in our dilemma. God is with us, in us, and working through us as we yield to His Spirit and choose to do what we "know-in-our-knower" pleases Him.

We must understand hardships will come. We are going to be hurt. Billy Graham was right. This journey with Jesus is not a walk in the park. Rather, it is a march on a battlefield. Unexpected disappointments and losses come with the territory. We cannot control much of what happens to us in this life, but we are responsible for how we respond. Will life's challenges make us "bitter" or, with God's help, make us "better"? We decide.

As the brilliant scientist Dr. Caroline Leaf reminds us, "Our mind has dominion over our brain." God has given us the ability to take inventory of our own thinking and, with His help, adjust our own attitudes.

AA meetings are filled with men and women who have, at one time or another, fallen to the "poor-mes." Poor me, poor me, pour me another drink. I know this is true because I was one of them! Although I have been sober for forty years, I still have bouts of "stinkin' thinkin'."

Regardless of what this world or the devil hits us with, we must not quit. Perseverance is a pearl of great worth. We must not quit.

For years, when I was a young Christian, I wrestled with the questions: "Do we choose God, or does God choose us?" and "Once we are saved, are we always saved, or can we lose it?"

I found the answer to the first question is "yes." We choose God, and He chooses us.

For many years, I wrestled with Matthew 22:14, where Jesus says, "For many are invited, but few are chosen." I heard many sermons on the topic, but the proposed explanations never really resonated with me. I always felt like there was some greater meaning I needed to discover.

Then, as casually as someone asking, "please pass the salt," the riddle was solved in my spirit as I heard a preacher share a vision she had. She said she had a vision of a large crowd of people walking away from the Lord. He called out to the crowd to turn around and come to Him. Some, not all, turned and looked at Him. To those who turned and looked His way, He pointed and said, "You and you and you…come to Me."

Many were called. Few were chosen.

In the same way, an even greater riddle for me was this business of "once saved, always saved." For years, I studied this and pondered this question. I discovered this debate has probably been going on since Jesus' encounter with "doubting Thomas" and the rich young ruler. It has been an ongoing debate and point of separation between denominations throughout church history up until this present time.

Many church fathers, much more brilliant than I, have fiercely defended their convictions on the matter. John Wesley was a powerhouse for the Lord and a staunch Arminian. He believed we could certainly lose our salvation. George Whitfield, a contemporary and fellow Oxford grad of Wesley, was a Calvinist and held firmly to the belief, "once saved, always saved."

Although these two men disagreed strongly theologically, they maintained a healthy respect for one another. So much so, in fact, they agreed that for whoever died first, the surviving friend would preach the other's funeral. This actually came to pass. When George Whitfield went to be with the Lord, John Wesley preached at his funeral.

As heartwarming as this act of true friendship was, it didn't solve the riddle for me. Once we're saved, are we always saved, or can we lose it?

Martin Luther's position on the subject almost gave me peace concerning the matter, but not entirely. Theologians describe Luther as being neither a Calvinist nor an Arminian. Luther's conclusion was simply, "Teach like an Arminian, live like a Calvinist." That will preach, as they say, but it didn't really answer the question or solve the riddle.

The pearl of wisdom I discovered regarding this issue surprised me as much as it blessed me. I pray it blesses you as well.

In the 1980s, Jean and I attended a church called Shiloh Covenant Fellowship. The pastor was a brilliant anointed Messianic Jewish man. God used Pastor Randy to impart into our lives in many ways. One Sunday morning, Pastor Randy broached the subject of eternal security. The story he shared to illustrate his convictions on the matter brought me peace and resolution, which has lasted more than forty years.

He shared the story of a wealthy rancher who lived out west in the 1800s. This wealthy rancher had only one child, a daughter. This daughter was the apple of her daddy's eye. She was the spitting image of her late mother, who the rancher also adored.

The young woman grew up to be quite bright and ambitious. When the time came for her to choose a college, she chose one in the eastern part of the country. To ensure her safe travel, the wealthy rancher put up generous prize money to be awarded to the stagecoach driver who could demonstrate the greatest skill.

Word spread far and wide of this stagecoach driving contest. The day of the contest arrived, and many young stagecoach drivers lined up in hopes of winning the lucrative assignment.

The first contestant started with a shot. Up the side of the mountain he went, displaying great skill and courage as he negotiated the arduous twists and turns of the narrow mountain path.

The second contestant followed with even more skill. His horses were more vibrant, and he made the trek up the mountain and back with such speed all the onlookers thought he would surely win the competition.

The third stagecoach driver wowed the crowd even more than the second. Some gasped as he pushed his horses and stagecoach to the limits as he took turns on two wheels at times but maintained control of his rig. All in the curios audience thought this skilled driver was sure to win the contest.

The next contestant was quite unimpressive. This stagecoach driver did not demonstrate near the level of skill and courage as the earlier contestants.

He slowly drove his coach up the mountain and back in a most casual manner. He stayed so far away from the challenging turns that onlookers couldn't even see him or witness what level of skill he possessed.

The crowd was agog when, upon his slow trek across the finish line, the wealth rancher exclaimed, "You're the man! You're the man I wish to hire to carry my precious daughter east."

Upon hearing Pastor Randy share this story, a Shalom peace came over me as I made a most surprising discovery concerning the question, "Once saved, always saved?" I discovered the problem is not in coming to the correct answer. The problem is it is a bad question! *Boom!* Drop the mic!

The rancher in the above story was awarded the father's trust not because he "pushed the limits" with great skill and daring. He won the father's trust because he was determined not to press the limits and see just how far he could push his stagecoach without going off the mountain!

Imagine if, when I fell in love with my Jean, I proposed to her by saying, "Sweetheart, I love you and want to marry you, but how far will you allow me to stray and still want to be my wife? How many other women will you allow me to have and still be my wife?"

When we really look closely at the "once saved, always saved" question, it really is just as ridiculous.

My pearl of discovery was not found in answering the question. It was realized by eliminating the silly question! I discovered a much better question: "Do you love Jesus?"

## Faith Challenge Questions

- Have you experienced stinkin' thinkin'?

- Have you ever questioned your salvation?

- Has Jesus brought you through a valley?

- Have you been on a mountaintop?

- Do you love Jesus? If so, why?

# A Pearl of Perseverance

## Never Quit

"Therefore, since we are surrounded by such a great cloud of witnesses ...let us run" (Hebrews 12:1).

Our daughter Connie was a true cross-country champion. With her ponytail keeping rhythm like a metronome, Connie ran like the autumn wind. Ranked number four in Hillsborough County, Florida, our *cum laude* grad of the University of South Florida always gave her all. She was poetry in motion.

*Daughter, Pastor Connie preaching with fire*

"Go, Connie, go!" I would yell from the crowd as she ran with all her heart to the finish line. I cherish the many special memories we share of races so well run.

Amid the stockpile of trophies and medals hides a seventh-place ribbon, her reward for her greatest race. She was in third place with a half-mile to go when she sprained her ankle badly due to a slight misstep. She kept running, but now with a limp. Soon she was in fourth place and then dropped to fifth place. "Go, Connie, go!"

With just a quarter-mile to go, she fell into sixth place. Grimacing in pain as she crossed the finish line in seventh place, her ankle was swollen larger than a softball. We immediately rushed our faltering track star to the hospital. Thank God it was just a bad sprain.

While waiting to be discharged from the emergency room, Coach Goff arrived with her seventh-place ribbon. "Connie, that was the best race you ever ran. You didn't give up. You didn't quit!" Yes! It was her best race indeed. She didn't give up. She didn't quit.

Life is full of hidden missteps, and good people stumble unexpectedly. Divorce, loss of loved ones, financial setbacks, and the like can trip even the best of us. Some days we run effortlessly. Some days we run with a limp.

But we run!

God's great cloud of witnesses surrounds us, cheering us to "press on!" We don't give up. We don't quit. No, we must never give up. We must never quit!

# CHAPTER EIGHTEEN:

# ADVENTURE AND DISCOVERY

*"The art of teaching is the art of assisting discovery."*

**Mark Van Doren**

Adventure and discovery often go hand in hand. This was certainly the case when Jean and I traveled to Israel. This trip of a lifetime came to us as we were enjoying the afterglow of our friends' wedding. Bill and May were married on a beautiful clear day at Clearwater Beach. It was a picture-postcard perfect kind of a day. The warm breeze blowing in off the Atlantic Ocean was delightful, and the waves crashing on the beach seemed unusually playful.

A couple of the elders at Bill and May's church approached us and said, "We're going to Israel again, and we'd like you guys to come with us."

We were flattered by their invitation. However, we were not at a place in our lives where this was financially feasible. So, we graciously declined.

With big smiles on their faces, this couple persisted. "You don't understand," they said. "All you have to do is show up. We will take care of all of your expenses."

This precious couple had been to Israel four times in as many years. Instead of going again themselves, they wanted someone else to experience this supernatural trip.

Of all the amazing sights we saw during our sojourn to the Holy Lands, and there were many, nothing was more beautiful than the joy on the faces of this godly couple cheering us on as we boarded our plane for departure. Their faces were beaming with joy. Even their body language demonstrated what Jesus must have meant when He said, "It is more blessed to give than to receive" (Acts 20:35).

Our trip from Tampa to Israel took twenty-four hours, door to door. It was quite a trek. The excitement of what awaited us seemed to diminish the impact of our long flight, complete with lengthy layovers and a seven-hour time difference.

On the day we arrived in Israel, we witnessed a beautiful bright rainbow. It was as if the Lord Himself was "putting a bow" on this incredible gift we were receiving.

We had been told going to Israel would forever change how we read the Bible. Those who had gone before us promised the Scriptures would become like a "pop-up book." They suggested we would come away with new insights and understanding of the places referenced in the Bible and the culture of the Jewish people. We found their predictions to be spot on.

We were a bit surprised to learn this was no leisurely stroll-in-the-park vacation. Our group leader, a brilliant Jewish woman by the name of Yael, was determined to pack as much into our eight days as humanly possible.

We greeted each day early with a delicious breakfast and then boarded the bus by 7:30 a.m. From sunrise to sunset, we took in the incredible sights and sounds of Israel.

We stood on Mt. Nebo, where Moses stood to look over the Promised Land. The Lord allowed Moses to see the Promised Land but, because of disobedience, was forbidden to enter.

In light of this sobering fact, it was quite humbling to board our bus and ride down to Jericho. We were agog as we stood by the ruins of the walls of Jericho, where Joshua and his friends had participated in the miraculous.

Each place we went to was just as amazing. We prayed where Jesus stood to deliver His Sermon on the Mount. We ventured out on the Sea of Galilee, where Jesus and Peter walked on water.

One of the pearls of discovery I found quite intriguing took place at lunch after we came in from our boat ride on the Sea of Galilee. The lunch special of the day at the restaurant was a dish appropriately named "St. Peter Fish." It was fried tilapia, served with its head still attached, of course.

We learned that, after giving birth, the mother tilapia protects her newborn babies by carrying them in her mouth for several days. When the time is right, the mother tilapia spits her babies out of her mouth. Understandably, the newly evicted babies diligently try to swim back in their mommy's mouth. To prevent the baby tilapia from reentering, the mother tilapia puts whatever shiny object she can find into her mouth and keeps it there for days.

It is believed this practice of the tilapia putting something shiny in its mouth is why Peter was able to "catch a fish with a gold coin in its mouth" per Jesus' instructions. Hence, the name "St. Peter Fish."

Digging a bit deeper into this "St. Peter Fish" discovery, it is interesting to note that sometimes Jesus does something only one time. I wonder how many industrious fishermen went tilapia fishing, in search of a similar bounty, after Peter's golden catch.

Perhaps some of Peter's close friends tried to walk on water after he decided to become a "wet water walker" instead of a "dry boat sitter" during his famous stormy encounter with Jesus.

What about weddings at Cana after the famous celebration where Jesus turned water into wine? Could the *maître d*'s have attempted to duplicate Jesus' first miracle?

Some things God does "one time." The Walls of Jericho fell one time from trumpet blasts; the Red Sea was parted one time; David killed a giant one time; the widow at Nain had one funeral halted by the Master; the woman with the alabaster box broke it one time.

The Bible speaks of one virgin birth, one sinless man who was baptized, crucified, and rose one time.

Praise God for His unmerited favor and habitual grace. Some things God repeatedly does, like waking us up every morning or forgiving our shortcomings and sins. The expressions of God's love and amazing grace are as countless as they are glorious.

Yet, when we realize God's actual grace can manifest in specific "one-time" ways in our life, it fosters a spirit of gratitude and adventure.

So, it was throughout our eight days in Israel. Every hour of every day, we were keenly aware that this was a trip of a lifetime.

Kneeling to pray in the Garden of Gethsemane, where Jesus sweated blood before the cross, was unforgettable. They say the olive trees there live more than 2,000 years. Touching those trees which Jesus may have touched with His loving, healing hands was surreal.

It was an unimaginable joy to walk where Jesus walked.

As we traveled from one historic landmark to the next, our tour guide, Yael, would often share some history and perhaps an insight about what we were witnessing. It quickly became clear that Yael was not at all a typical tour guide like one may find leading excursions at Disney World or Bush Gardens. As a matter of fact, Yael was brilliant. We later learned she had earned not one but two PhDs. Although Yael was not a Christian, her commentary revealed a great knowledge of both the Old and New Testaments.

One pearl of revelation she shared radically altered my understanding of one of my favorite scriptures.

As our bus rolled along beside the Judaea wilderness, we peered out of the windows and observed a terrain similar to that of Arizona. The land was flat and open and desert-like. In the distance, we saw shepherds leading small flocks of sheep.

Yael pointed to the distant shepherds and said, "Do you remember how the psalmist said, 'He makes me lie down in green pastures'?" She went on to explain in the original language, the Hebrew words for "green pastures" actually meant "patchy green areas."

Up until that moment, whenever I read or heard the twenty-third Psalm, I would imagine lush "green pastures" like one would find as they traveled through North Carolina or Tennessee. Now, as we looked out and saw this vast desert land with its small patches of grass, the Psalm took on a whole new meaning.

It was clear these shepherds were leading their sheep through the dry arid places to bring them to sparse patchy green areas of grass. Isn't that exactly what the Good Shepherd does in our lives? As we journey through life, we find ourselves pressing on, at times, through dry arid arduous places.

It would be wonderful if our walk with Jesus was always butterflies and rainbows, but that's not the reality. Jesus wasn't kidding in John 16:33 when He said, "In this world you will have trouble. But take heart! I have overcome the world."

The psalmist also warns us about life's challenges in Psalm 34:19: "The righteous person may have many troubles, but the Lord delivers him from them all."

In life, we will have trouble and loss, disappointment, and unexpected betrayal. However, like those diligent young shepherds we witnessed from the comfort of our tour bus, our great shepherd leads us through the dry places and brings us to those "patchy green areas" of refreshment.

In his book, *The Purpose Driven Life*, Rick Warren says, "We are products of our past, but we do not have to be prisoners of it."

In the midst of life's challenges, we joy in knowing our Shepherd brings us through every obstacle. He turns every test into a testimony and gives us a message through every mess. Our part is staying close to the Shepherd.

Peter warns us in 1 Peter 5:8 that "[our] enemy the devil prowls around like a roaring lion looking for someone to devour."

Have you ever watched a lion hunt in one of those nature shows on TV? The lion rarely charges the middle of the flock. No, the lion usually stalks the one lone sheep or antelope that is away from the pack. As we say in *Via de Cristo*, "An isolated Christian is a paralyzed Christian." This is quite true. It is also true that an isolated Christian is a vulnerable Christian.

Our adversary can't create anything new. He himself is a created being. Yet, he has been in this business of "deceive, divide, and conquer" for a long time. He is quite skilled at his old tricks.

The best and wisest thing any Christian can do is "stay close to the Shepherd." He leads us in His paths of righteousness for His name's sake. He prepares a table before us even in the presence of our enemies. He anoints our head with oil and overflows our cup with His purpose and presence as we walk closely with Him, one day at a time.

As I mentioned, our tour guide in Israel was not a Christian. Furthermore, before embarking on our trip to the Holy Lands, we were instructed not to "proselytize." In plain English, we were warned if we tried to win converts to Jesus on the streets of Israel, we would be thrown in jail.

As we traveled all over this magnificent land and enjoyed our brilliant tour guide, my heart grew more and more burdened to share the good news with Yael. Knowing that doing so would be a serious infraction, I held back. As I prayed for Yael, the Holy Spirit reminded me how our Jesus specializes in making a way where there is no way. I watched and prayed every day for some opportunity to point Yael to Jesus. Again, our awesome God proved Himself faithful.

At every holy site we visited, our lead pastor assigned one of the ministers on the team to share a scripture and small meditation. Jean did a beautiful job sharing her scripture and message as we gathered in Bethlehem. I was asked to share as we explored the Mount of Ascension, the place where Jesus left His friends and ascended into heaven.

Yael was standing close by as our group gathered at this holy site. I seized the moment to witness to her by looking directly at her and reciting a poem I had written right after I had been born again.

My heart quietly leaped for joy the next morning as we boarded our tour bus. Yael greeted each of us as she did every morning. As I stepped on the bus, she shook my hand a little longer than expected, looked me in the eyes, and said, "I enjoyed your poem yesterday."

Will we see Yael in heaven? I pray we will. God was faithful to make a way for me to plant a seed. Many times since then, I have remembered Yael and watered that seed with prayers.

In 1 Corinthians 3:6, Paul encourages us by saying, "I planted the seed, Apollos watered it, but God has been making it grow."

God often works in ways we don't understand. Truly, His ways are different than our ways.

I discovered one such unexpected blessing the day

our team visited the Pool of Bethesda. We learn in John chapter 5 that this is the place where Jesus confronted a man who had been paralyzed for thirty-eight years.

The question Jesus asked the man echoes through the centuries, "Do you want to get well?" The paralyzed man never did answer Jesus. In fact, he seemed to blame others for his condition. Regardless, Jesus healed him, and the Pool of Bethesda has been famous ever since.

As with so many of the holy places in Israel where miracles took place, a beautiful church was erected next to the Pool.

Before our team began the mile-long walk through the Old City of Jerusalem to the Pool of Bethesda, our lead pastor warned us about pickpockets and purse-snatchers in this area. Pastor Bill told me he would keep an eye on the team from the front of the group and asked me to serve as our rear guard. As soon as we began our march, my foot slipped off one of the large cobblestones, and I twisted my ankle very badly.

Because I was the last one in our group, no one, except Jean, saw how futilely I was hobbling along just to keep up. I remember wondering just what in the world would I do if one of these notorious purse-snatchers showed up on my watch. There was no way I could chase them. I could barely walk.

We reached the church without incident and enjoyed a beautiful time of worship before going next door to visit the famous pool. As we exited the church, a woman was complaining about having a terrible headache. She asked the group if anyone had any Tylenol. Her request was met with complete silence. No one had any.

I raised my voice and said, "I have some oil; we can anoint you and pray."

The woman with the headache and most of the folks around her looked confused and perplexed. Anointing with oil and praying for healing was not a practice most of our group was familiar with. Our lead pastor thought it was a good idea and encouraged the reluctant woman to accept my offer. She stood with rigor mortis-like stillness as I rubbed a little anointing oil on her head and prayed for the Lord to lift this headache off her.

As soon as we said a collective "amen," we began to walk towards the beautiful Pool of Bethesda. I was watching the woman with the headache very closely, hoping to see or hear some sign she was experiencing some relief. There was none.

As we were walking, listening to this old gal continue to complain about her headache, I made a most unexpected discovery. My foot was 100 percent healed. I don't mean it felt somewhat better. I mean to tell you that my ankle was suddenly and completely healed. There are no magic wands or silver bullets available to us in our journey with Jesus. However, there are principles that govern the kingdom of God just as sure as the law of gravity governs the earth.

As we reach out to others, we are healed.

To this day, when I remember our supernatural adventure through the Holy Lands, being baptized in the Jordan River and being healed at the Pool of Bethesda are two gems from Jesus I will always cherish.

Would Jesus have healed my ankle even if I didn't step out of my comfort zone to anoint the woman with a headache? Perhaps. We'll never know.

One thing I do know. As we reach out to others, we are healed.

## Faith Challenge Questions

- When have you seen great joy on someone's face?

- Can you recall a "once in a lifetime" blessing?

- What dry wilderness has Jesus brought you through?

- When have you reached out to someone and received a "boomerang" blessing?

# A Pearl of a Journey

## We Walk Where Jesus Walked

*"Whoever claims to live in him must live as Jesus did" (1 John 2:6).*

While in Israel, we walked where Jesus walked. It was surreal. It was holy. We prayed in Bethlehem and touched the olive trees of Gethsemane. We sang in Cana, climbed the Sermon Mount, and gazed at Calvary. We were awe-struck on the shores of Galilee as we heard the Spirit whisper quietly, "Feed My sheep."

*Jim & Jean at the empty tomb*

Nazareth, Capernaum, Jerusalem, and Golgotha left their mark on our very souls. The Bible will never be the same since we walked where Jesus walked. Yes, we walked where Jesus walked!

Though many miles from Bethlehem now, we are close to Jesus still. Walking with the homeless, the orphan, the prisoner, we walk where Jesus walked.

May we always be covered in the dust of our Rabbi as we walk where Jesus walked! Yes! We walk where Jesus walked!

# CHAPTER NINETEEN:

# THE KING'S PARTY

*"The pessimist sees difficulty in every opportunity.*
*The optimist sees opportunity in every difficulty."*
**Winston Churchill**

There is a lot of real estate between the Mount of Ascension in Israel and death row in Raiford, Florida. Yet, we have witnessed Jesus in both places with unmistakable blessings.

Yes, He does make us lay down in green pastures, and, yes, He does walk with us through the valley of the shadow of death.

In our journey, some of God's greatest blessings have been what I describe as unexpected blessings. We received another one of God's unexpected blessings a couple of weeks ago as we were "pre-prayering" for our Christmas Eve outreach to Putnam Prison in East Palatka, Florida.

It's hard for me to process we have spearheaded Christmas Eve outreaches to Putnam Prison every year for the last twenty years. Over the years, these outreaches have morphed into something quite special. Every Christmas Eve outreach at Putnam Prison has truly been a mega-blessed mountaintop experience. We have witnessed well over a thousand brothers-in-blue get saved during these celebrations, and every time, God touches the heart and life of every team member in an unforgettable way.

To give you some perspective on our most recent unexpected blessing as it relates to Putnam Prison, perhaps sharing how God initially opened the door to Putnam C. I. will help. It certainly was a "God thing" we were not expecting.

We planted Higher Ground Ministries in September of 1999 and immediately began holding church services at the Upper Room coffee house in DeLand, Florida.

In an effort to get the gospel out and spread the word about our new non-traditional outreach-focused church, we had a live one-hour radio program on WAPN Radio in Daytona Beach.

Hosting the live radio show was quite comical because, in spite of my many years working in radio and TV, I had no idea how to properly use the technical equipment in the control room. We could spiritualize the situation and say Jean and I were "walking by faith," but the truth is we were flying by the seat of our pants.

Regardless, we had fun. Some of the guests we

interviewed live on the air are now in heaven or back in prison.

As I mentioned, this one-hour weekly radio program was always done live. However, on one occasion, Jean and I prerecorded a program due to a ministry commitment at Zephyrhills Prison across the state.

At the end of every radio program, Jean and I always invited listeners to call in for prayer requests. During the one-week program, when Jean and I weren't there, our son, Jimmy, and brother-in-law, Scott, agreed to sit outside of the control room to man the phones in case someone called in for prayer.

Sure enough, as the pre-recorded program aired and the call for prayer went out, the phone rang. A man named Charlie was listening to the program with his only earthly possessions, a small transistor radio.

Charlie had just been released from Putnam Prison and was in bed at a hotel in Daytona Beach. When he heard the invitation to receive prayer, he jotted down the telephone number, got up, got dressed, and went downstairs to use the payphone on the street in front of his hotel.

When Charlie called in, Jimmy and Scott gladly spoke with him, prayed with him, and bid Charlie a good night. Charlie, encouraged by the heartfelt prayers, went back upstairs, got undressed, got back into bed, and tuned back in to hear the rest of the radio program.

In the meantime, Jimmy and Scott were kicking themselves. "We should have invited Charlie to church," they exclaimed. "We talked with him and prayed with him, but we didn't invite him to join us for church tomorrow," they lamented.

As Jimmy and Scott sat in the lobby of WAPN Radio, going back and forth about what they should have done, Scott made a most unusual and unexpected observation. He somehow, by the grace of God, noticed the slight humming sound of the small window unit air conditioner in the control room was coming across the airwaves of the radio program being pumped into the lobby. An even greater manifestation of the actual grace of God was how these two serendipitous prayer warriors connected the dots and concluded the microphone in the control room must be live.

Neither of these men had ever been inside of a control room at a radio station. Furthermore, it is a cardinal rule in broadcasting never to leave a microphone on when it is not in use.

Compelled by their overwhelming desire to somehow reach out to Charlie, Jimmy and Scott snuck into the control room through the unexpectedly unlocked door. "Charlie, if you're out there and you hear me, call us back here at the radio station," Jimmy heralded.

Charlie had just snuggled back into his cozy bed, no doubt enjoying the serenity of a bed void of the constant cacophony of prison noise. Charlie heard the clarion call and, for a second time, got up, got dressed, went downstairs, and called the radio station from the payphone in front of his hotel.

Jimmy and Scott offered to pick him up the next morning and bring him to church. He gladly accepted their invitation, and for the next few weeks, Charlie H. was a most welcomed and enthusiastic guest at our Higher Ground Sunday celebrations.

After every Sunday service, Charlie made a beeline right to me. "You need to call Chaplain Dave at Putnam Prison. He would like to meet you." Again and again, after every Sunday service, Charlie insisted it was important we contact Chaplain Dave at Putnam C. I.

Although we had never heard of Putnam Prison or East Palatka, Florida for that matter, in response to Charlie's dogged persistence, I picked up the phone and called Chaplain Dave. It was a divine connection for sure.

Over the next twenty years, up until this present moment, Putnam Prison has been a fruitful mission field. Throughout these two-plus decades, we have held six to ten outreach services each year.

Because of the many prisoner transfers and men who are newly incarcerated, we have enjoyed reaching new souls in every service. I understand we are "in the book of Acts" and not in "the book of Numbers," but it is heartwarming to look back and see, in every service, that many souls were saved.

During the first few years, the brother-in-blue running the sound from the back of the large chapel at Putnam Prison was a big worshipful guy. His name is James, but they called him "Gator." He was serving a forty-year sentence for shooting his ex-wife six times.

Without intending to and not even knowing he had been released from prison, we walked right by Gator while attending Chaplain Dave & Carol's wedding in Interlocken, Florida. "Well, go on and walk right by me then," Gator said with a strong Southern drawl.

*Bringing BK Whoppers to Putnam Prison on Christmas Eve*

It was another one of God's unexpected blessings. What was even more unexpected was the close friendship and ministry partnership God blessed Jean and me and Gator and his beautiful wife, Kim, with. They have become very dear lifelong friends and powerful ministry companions.

While Gator and I were talking one day, not long after he had become a free man, he said, "Jim, you know what men miss most when they are inside the razor wire?" he asked rhetorically. "Food!" He went on to share his dream that one day we could bring Burger King Whoppers to our brothers-in-blue at Putnam C. I.

I called Chaplain Dave and asked what he thought of the idea. "That's what I like about you, Brissey; you're as crazy as I am," was his response.

Somewhat pleadingly, I said, "Well, Chap, Scripture says 'we have not because we ask not.' Could you at least ask the Warden?"

I have known Chap for more than twenty years now. Yet, I had never heard him so excited as he did when he returned my call the next day.

"He said, yes!" Chaplain Dave announced with glee. "The Warden approved our request for you to bring Burger King Whoppers in for Christmas Eve!"

The first person I called to announce this unexpected blessing was Gator. We rejoiced like kids at Christmas.

During the first couple of (pre-Whopper) Christmas Eve services at Putnam, the chapel would be packed out with standing room only and more than 200 inmates in attendance. Now, with the news that "the king was coming" (Burger King, that is), it was necessary to hold two services to accommodate the more than 450 prisoners attending.

Each year the Burger King in East Palatka, Florida "knocked it out of the park," having 500 BK Whoppers hot and ready for pick up at the appointed time.

Words really can't describe what it is like to witness what God does in the chapel at Putnam Prison on Christmas

Eve. It is more than special. It is holy.

While in the wilderness, the Israelites complained about their constant menu of manna. The Lord heard their cries and rained down quail as an unexpected blessing.

At Putnam Prison, God honored the dream of one ex-convict. For the last fifteen Christmas Eves, every man on the compound, including the correctional officers, has enjoyed a fresh Burger King Whopper, a cinnamon bun, and a cup of hot coffee. What a mighty God we serve.

*"500 BK Whoppers, please!"*

Before long, Gator took it upon himself to raise funds to cover the costs of our Christmas Eve outreaches. This unexpected blessing has overflowed with a surplus, helping to fuel other outreaches

At the beginning of this chapter, I mentioned one specific unexpected blessing we received while pre-prayering for this year's Christmas Eve outreach to Putnam Prison.

To give you context, I must digress back to our death row friend, Manny Valle. I shared earlier how Manny gave his life to Jesus and how over the next four subsequent years, we became good friends. I also shared how for seven years, on the anniversary of Manny's execution, Gator and I went to death row, sang "Amazing Grace," and invited the 330 men on the row to receive Jesus.

Every year during this outreach in Manny's honor, about a dozen or so men on the row would pray with us. One of the men who prayed to receive Christ is Tom M. Tom has lived on death row for nine years.

As I was on my way to facilitate the graduation ceremony for Cycle 9 of our Higher Ground School of Ministry at Putnam Prison, I swung by the post office. There I discovered an unexpected Christmas card from Tom M. Along with a note of encouragement for our upcoming Christmas Eve outreach at Putnam, Tom included a $1,000 money order.

This unexpected blessing not only put us over the top to cover the cost of the outreach, the message to our brothers-in-blue on Christmas Eve that a man on death row helped to pay for the Christmas Eve Whoppers added tremendous impact to our outreach.

More than a hundred men stood and committed their life to Jesus Christ on Christmas Eve, 2021, at Putnam

Prison. This miracle of grace happened, in part, because of the unexpected blessing from a convicted murderer on death row who reached out from his six by eight inches cell (where he has resided twenty-three hours a day for the last nine years.)

Less than two weeks after Tom M. sent the unexpected blessing of $1,000 to help with the Whoppers, he received an unexpected blessing of his own. He just received news that his victim's family will not oppose his lawyer's motion to move him off death row. His appeal has been granted, and, as I write this, Tom is being moved off death row and into general population.

# Faith Challenge Questions

- How has God blessed you?

- How has God blessed your family?

- How has God blessed your friends?

- When have you received an unexpected blessing?

# CHAPTER TWENTY:

# RED MAN, WHITE MAN

*"Keep your face always toward the sunshine – and
shadows will fall behind you."*

**Walt Whitman**

As we continue in our journey with Jesus, we learn to
question what we hear and look at what we see through
different lenses.

This pearl of wisdom proved helpful as we "pre-
prayered" to bring a mission team to reach out to the
Lakota Indians in Bullhead, South Dakota.

The couple who hosted our team were former drug
dealers from Miami. God had gotten ahold of them,
changed their lives, and moved their family to Bullhead,
South Dakota, to minister to the Native Americans at
Standing Rock Indian Reservation.

One could not help but recognize God's wisdom
in calling these ex-drug dealers to the Lakota Indian

population. The statistics for alcoholism, drug addiction, child and spousal abuse, as well as suicide among these Native Americans are staggering.

Approximately 40 percent of these families are crippled by addiction, child abuse, and spousal abuse. The suicide rate is nearly three times the national average.

Knowing this couple had hosted many mission teams over the past several years, Jean asked, "About how many salvations have your other mission teams witnessed?"

"None," they answered. "The Red Man doesn't receive from the White Man."

Although we had never reached out to Native Americans before, we didn't believe this report for a minute. If we had, we would have just stayed home.

In Isaiah 53:1, God asks, "Who has believed our message ...?" Whether it is in ministry or in our daily life, we are often faced with a choice. Will we believe man's report, or will we believe the Lord?

As we soaked this outreach in prayer, we chose to believe God's promise that He is no respecter of persons. We declared His Word would not return void. We "knew-in-our-knowers" God is not willing that any should perish. Red, brown, black, or white, they are precious in His sight.

Over a few months, the team consisting of a dozen outreach ministers came together. Jean recruited most of them to participate in an interpretive dance she had choreographed to the song "God's Not Dead" by the

Newsboys. She tirelessly taught each member their steps.

Soon after arriving at the Standing Rock Indian Reservation, we invited the precious but rambunctious Native American children to come to learn the dance. Dozens of kids came to dance practice every day. We soon had a whole new appreciation for the phrase "behaving like wild Indians."

Many of the drug-addicted, alcoholic Lakota fathers abused their kids and made them say they received their injuries by "falling down the stairs." These children, many of which displayed fresh bruises from "falling down the stairs," were very challenging. We resorted to blackmailing the kids and paying each one a dollar if they could make it through dance practice. Jean exercised great patience and worked diligently teaching those kids who were willing and able.

Our team met for worship and prayer every morning before dance practice. After dance practice, we broke into two-person teams and went door to door throughout the Standing Rock Indian Reservation.

We invited everyone to a revival service scheduled to take place at the end of the week in front of the Lakota Pow Wow Grounds. Our revival was to be held in front of the Pow Wow Grounds because only those individuals who were 100 percent Lakota Indian were allowed to set foot on the hallowed Pow Wow Grounds.

As far as our hosts' proclamation that "the Red Man doesn't receive from the White Man," nothing could have been further from the truth. Each day, as our team went door to door, dozens of precious "red men and women" prayed and invited Jesus into their hearts.

Word spread like wildfire throughout the Reservation that these Jesus people from Florida had love. The response of the Lakota people to God's love in our team and to the gospel was astounding. We were like fishermen watching fish jump into our boat.

Our granddaughter, Elicia, went door to door with Jean & me one day. Her dad had given her a beautiful bracelet to give away. "You will know who to give it to at the time," he told her. The bracelet was engraved with the words, "No weapon formed against you will prosper."

We encountered a Lakota couple with one small child, whose twin had recently "fallen down the stairs" and died. Elicia prayed for the child as Jean and I prayed for the parents. After we said, "Amen," this pitiful grieving mom was touched by God's love as Elicia was prompted to give her the special bracelet.

Another day, Jean & I encountered a couple who shared that very day was the one-year anniversary of their beautiful teenage daughter committing suicide. We all cried and prayed as this precious couple was born again in their living room.

One of our team members had an encounter we still laugh about today.

Our team members, Malachi and Angel, were teenagers and new believers at the time. Soon after, they approached a nearby mobile home and knocked, the front door opened, and a big cloud of marijuana smoke billowed out.

As they were telling this couple about Jesus and His love, Angel innocently said, "You know, you guys are probably going to get the munchies soon, and we have a lot of snacks at the clubhouse for you!" LOL.

Before the week was out, the husband did respond to the gospel and gave his life to the Lord.

The week was filled with wonderful testimonies and many heartwarming encounters. Truly, God's love never fails.

Thirty minutes before the big finale revival meeting was to begin, word came from the Lakota Board of Elders that our team was invited to minister on the actual Pow Wow Grounds. This was unheard of.

It was so unusual; some of the white folks in attendance freaked out as we began walking onto the Pow Wow Grounds. "Get off, get off...that's holy ground," some shouted.

*Jean and team at Standing Rock Indian Reservation, Bullhead, S.D.*

Jean's work teaching the kids and including the children in the beautifully choreographed interpretive dance softened the hearts of the Elders.

After a time of worship, Jean and the dance team (with many of the Lakota kids) "knocked it out of the park" right there in the middle of the holiest place in Standing Rock Indian Reservation. The Lord anointed this upbeat song and terrific choreography in a glorious way.

I was humbled to bring a message about "The Great Spirit" and how He sent His Son to save us. More than forty adult Lakota men and women answered the altar call and came forward to receive Jesus as Savior and Lord.

Several fell out in the Spirit as our team laid hands on them. One woman went home and immediately poured out all the alcohol in her house. One thirteen-year-old "bully of a child," who had been the most belligerent throughout the week, came up to me after the service was over.

"I prayed that prayer," he confided in me. "I asked Jesus to come into my heart."

I tell you the truth; I would have done all that we did just to hear that one precious, troubled, abused young man share those sincere words.

"The Red Man doesn't receive from the White Man." Really? My father-in-law's saying seemed almost prophetic. "Don't believe anything you hear and half of why you see!"

More than a hundred "red men and women" gave their hearts to Jesus that week. The response was so great that the hosts literally had to start a satellite church right there on Standing Rock Reservation. They named the church "Hope Rising Church."

Every year for the next several years, some on our team brought others and went back to minister at Hope Rising Church.

## Faith Challenge Questions

- When have you chosen to believe God's promise over something man told you?

- What unorthodox method have you used to further the gospel?

- When has God done something so great you almost can't believe your eyes?

- When have you enjoyed a good laugh during a ministry situation?

# A Pearl of Favor

# Shine

*"You will shine ...like stars" (Philippians 2:15).*

Stepping out of the van, our mission team of ten beheld a sky like none we had ever seen before. Midnight in rural South Dakota presented a sky resembling black velvet with a thousand shining diamonds scattered about by the hand of God. Magnificent!

The next morning came quickly as our team "pre-prayered" to bring the good news to the Lakota Indian people on Standing Rock Reservation in Bullhead, South Dakota. We had learned of the dismal demographics of these hurting people for whom addiction, child abuse, and suicide are the norm. We had also heard that the Indian people were resistant to the white man. Because of this, normally, very few salvations are recorded.

Armed with peanut butter and jelly sandwiches and the song of the Lord, we rode into Bullhead with a deep sense of purpose. We were a long way from Daytona Beach but so very close to the heart of God.

Our hearts burned with God's love as we went house to house with compassion and the power of the Holy Spirit. Many felt the Spirit of the living God and were compelled to receive Him as King. By day three, these precious people were jumping in the boat. The Holy Spirit flowed like a fresh mountain stream as scores of Native Americans received Christ in four short days. Wow! As spiritual people, they needed to feel God's presence to know that Jesus is real.

The surnames of these precious people sounded like storybook titles: Red Bear, Yellow Earrings, Running Hawk, and Elk Nation. Their life stories would break the hardest of hearts. We prayed with many, young and old, men and women, boys and girls. So many of them sad, so many hurting. Many hearts were healed from the ravages of loved ones lost to drugs and suicide. The Balm of Gilead had a great impact on Standing Rock Reservation.

God's not dead! He's surely alive!

*Jim preaching on the Pow Wow Grounds,*
*Standing Rock Indian Reservation, Bullhead, S.D.*

# CHAPTER TWENTY-ONE:

# UNEXPECTED BLESSINGS

*"Gratitude is not only the greatest of virtues, but the parent of all others."*

**Marcus Tullius Cicero**

Some pearls of discovery we make along life's journey are not gleeful ones. Such is the unfolding discovery that God's timing and our timing are often two very different things.

Isaiah 55:8 is a frequently quoted verse of Scripture. Here the prophet makes clear that God's ways are different than our ways. As we grow in Christ, we realize this more and more.

Scripture is full of many vivid examples. Abraham had his Ishmael before he and Sarah produced their Isaac. David fell with Bathsheba before they produced Solomon. I find it fascinating that Jesus came through the line of

Bathsheba as well as through the ancestral line of Rahab, the prostitute.

Certainly, we see how God's ways are different than our ways. The Gospels and, ultimately, the cross, illuminate this truth quite brightly.

Jesus' choices for disciples were as surprising as they were unorthodox. Fishermen and tax collectors were not frequent guests of the religious ruling class in Jesus' day.

The scribes and the Pharisees (and the wouldn't-sees and couldn't-sees) must have laughed out loud at this rag-tag bunch when they first started making noise about this new faith.

There must have been a good bit of head-scratching and consternation even within the ranks of the twelve disciples Jesus called by name. Can you imagine being a fly on the wall when Jesus introduced Matthew to Peter? Perhaps it went something like:

"Hey, Simon, John, James.... Fellas, come over here and meet the newest member of our team. His name is Matthew. He's a tax collector."

Peter, James, and John were fishermen. They were hard-working men trying to feed their families. Tax collectors were notorious for exploiting the blue-collar workers of their day.

Peter was never accused of being someone who kept his thoughts or words to himself. What a colorful introduction he and Matthew must have enjoyed! Or how did the conversation go when Peter went home for dinner and told his wife about his new co-worker?

"How did things go today, honey?" Mrs. Peter might have asked.

"Well, the Rabbi surprised us again. He brought in a new guy named Matthew. He's a tax collector. Pass the peas, please!"

God's ways are, indeed, very different than our ways.

When Peter inquired about paying taxes, Jesus told him to go fishing and catch a fish with a gold coin in its mouth. When faced with a crowd of 5,000 hungry onlookers, Jesus fed them with a little boy's lunch.

The widow at Nain must have gone through a great deal of time, expense, and planning to honor her son with a proper funeral, only to have her plans turned upside down as Jesus halted the funeral procession and raised the young man from the dead.

Zacchaeus had an unexpected dinner guest. Bartimaeus saw things he never thought he would see. The Roman Centurion was surprised by grace. Peter walked on water. Pig farmers went out of business. Lazarus reunited with his sisters.

On and on it goes. The gospel is chock-full of examples of how different God's ways are from our ways. The greatest object lesson of all is, without a doubt, the cross.

Paul says it best in Galatians 6:14, "May I never except in the cross of our Lord Jesus Christ, through which the world has been crucified to me, and I to the world."

The most grotesque form of torture and murder ever concocted in the bowels of Hades is the way to life and peace for us who believe.

Discovering the vast differences between God's ways and our ways is evident to every believer. A first-year Bible student will certainly recognize this blinding flash of the obvious.

However, the timings of the Lord are quite a different matter. It can take years and years of walking with Jesus before one can appreciate what I mean when I say, "God is not in a hurry!"

Yes, we do serve an "on-time God." No, He's never late. But, by golly, He's never early either! His timing is very different than our timing.

In our culture, it is common for folks to go through four years of college to prepare for forty years of work in a particular occupation. Jesus trained thirty years for three years of ministry.

When Jean and I were first called to the ministry, we thought God meant "now." We would find ourselves in prophetic meetings, and various prophets would call us out and "give us a word," "You two are called to full-time ministry."

"Okay, Lord," I would pray. "We're ready."

In my spirit, the Lord would clearly say, "No, you're not ready."

Months would go by. Again, we would find ourselves in a church service, and ministers who were complete strangers would "call us out and give us the same word."

Again, I would pray. "Okay, Lord. We are ready."

And again, the Lord would say, "No, you are not ready."

This scenario repeated itself for fifteen years. During these years, we were involved in various forms of outreach and ministry, but the tugging on our hearts to launch into full-time ministry only grew stronger and stronger.

I began to imagine what a pregnant woman must feel like in her tenth month of pregnancy. Over these fifteen years, this "call" morphed from being exciting to redundant to frustrating to excruciating.

I remember one night walking out of the Colonnade Restaurant on a date night with Jean. After enjoying a delicious meal, we often walked down Bayshore Boulevard in Tampa. As we began talking about our call to full-time ministry, I found myself literally preaching to the fish in Tampa Bay. We joke around today, saying two mackerels were saved that night.

Hindsight is 20/20. Looking back now, after twenty-five-plus years have passed since we finally were launched into full-time ministry, two things are abundantly clear:

First, God was right. We were not ready when I thought we were ready, and second, what I wrongly interpreted as God being cruel in delaying our launch into full-time ministry was God being merciful.

God's Word exhorts us to "comfort those in any trouble with the comfort we ourselves receive from God" (2 Corinthians 1:4). This kingdom mandate is at the heartbeat of this book.

It is my prayer that through these ramblings and testimonies, my children, grandchildren, great-grandchildren, family, friends, and fellow Christ-followers may discover some pearls of insight to help comfort, counsel, and propel them onward and upward to higher ground in God.

Looking back, it is easy to see God's handiwork. Looking forward, we walk by faith and not by sight. As we do press on to the unique plan God has for each of us, we are wise to recognize and remind ourselves of this simple but profound truth. God is not in a hurry. His timing is different from our timing.

Before getting off of this soapbox and bringing this chapter to a close, I want to share one truer-to-life illustration.

In Ecclesiastes 11:1, Solomon, the wisest man who ever lived, said, "Ship your grain across the sea; after many days you may receive a return."

To fully appreciate what God did, you must have some context about what I'm going to share.

*My beautiful fiance, Jean*

Jean and I met on July 5, 1976. She had a yellow bikini. I had a blue Kawasaki. We fell in love, got pregnant, and on December 17 of the same year, we were married. Jean was nineteen going on sixteen, and I was twenty-two going on fifteen. We didn't know Jesus from a can of paint. We were as dumb as rocks and poor as dirt, but we loved each other and our baby-to-be.

By the amazing grace of God, we stumbled upon a pastor and church who gave us a beautiful wedding. Jean borrowed her friend's wedding gown. I spent the last $100 I had to rent a brown tuxedo. There has never been a more beautiful bride to walk an aisle as Jean.

However, one thing my bride didn't have that day was a diamond ring. We had purchased a couple of wedding bands to make things official, but there was no fiancé getting on his knee and presenting a diamond ring for Jean.

Our wedding plans were born during the doctor's visit when the OBGYN exclaimed, "Yep. You're pregnant."

Don't get me wrong, our precious daughter, Connie, was not expected, but she was never unwanted, not for one minute. This was a miracle of grace in light of the wholesale abortion craze going on in New York City at the time.

Abortion never entered our minds. We loved each other. We loved our baby. We were getting married and starting a family. However, we were doing so in a most abrupt and, in the eyes of Jean's old-fashioned Italian family, scandalous way.

Jean's dad was too ashamed to attend our wedding. Her uncle did that with an angry scowl on his face. "Dis guy betta love you," he barked at Jean seconds before walking his niece to the altar.

Other than my mom and sister, Roxie, none of my family attended our wedding either.

There was no fancy reception or celebration afterward. The church folks lovingly served bologna sandwiches and punch in the church's small fellowship hall for the handful of folks who came.

Jean and I couldn't care less about any of that. We

loved each other, and now we were husband and wife. Most folks probably didn't give us a snowball's chance in Hades of "making it."

However, looking back to that day more than forty-five years ago, the beautiful song the church soloist sang at our wedding turned out to be quite prophetic. "One Love for a Lifetime" will forever be "our song."

I don't know if the women who read this will understand as well as the men will, but I felt "less than" for not being able to put a diamond ring on my wife's finger. This was a constant unspoken secret, painful regret I carried. This secret shame in my heart was healed a few years later when Jean's grandmother passed away. Jean's mom gave Jean her grandmother's beautiful diamond ring. It was quite a special ring, not only because Jean was named after her grandmother, Jean, but also because Jean and I were graced to pray with Grandma Jean on her death bed. When we did, Grandma Jean gave us an unforgettable wink of faith when we asked if she was trusting Jesus for eternal life. Soon after, she went to heaven.

Countless times over the next few years, I would glance over at Jean's diamond ring and thank the Lord for healing my secret shame. Since coming to know Jesus a few years after our marriage, this was one of the greatest things the Lord had done in my life.

In the mid-eighties, a very popular song we sang in church was titled "Lord You Are More Precious than Silver." Some of the lyrics were, "Lord, you are more precious than silver. Lord, you are more costly than gold.

Lord, you are more beautiful than diamonds, and nothing I desire compares with you."

You can imagine my dismay when Jean leaned over to me in church after singing this song and whispered, "I think the Lord wants me to put my diamond ring on the offering plate."

"Please don't," I insisted. "At least wait until next week. Pray about it, and if you still feel strongly next Sunday, then okay."

I swallowed hard the following Sunday as I watched Jean secretly slip off her beautiful diamond ring and inconspicuously put it on the offering plate.

Money had nothing to do with my silent sense of loss. This ring was special. God had used it to bring deliverance to my secret shame, and now this diamond was gone. I wrestled with the Lord about this for the next few days. At the same time, our wedding anniversary was coming up, and I was wondering what anniversary gift I could get for Jean.

It dawned on me that the Lord had spoken to Jean about giving the ring, not me. I called our pastor and, in confidence, told him about the ring and asked if I could purchase it. He was very understanding but had already sold the ring to a local jeweler. I called the jeweler and, again, explained my hope of redeeming the ring. He informed me he had already removed the stone but graciously offered to put Jean's diamond in a new setting if I cared to purchase it.

On our wedding anniversary that year, I was overjoyed to put Jean's diamond on her finger again. Do you remember Solomon's promise about "casting your bread upon the water" and how he exhorts us that "after many days" it may return?

Fast forward to 2006. My dad's declining health required us to place Dad in assisted living. The unpleasant task of holding an estate sale to liquidate my dad's earthly possessions fell upon Jean and me.

The day came, and it was even more unpleasant than anticipated. Auctioning off dad's things and haggling with the bargain hunters in North Miami was tough. Jean did most of the bargaining while I hid out in the garage. I came in periodically to see how things were going. In doing so, I noticed one hardcore bargain hunter negotiating with Jean over this and that. I found this man to be particularly annoying. He milled about for about an hour and ended up spending seven dollars for a couple of small items, including a couple of wicker owl tchotchke items which Jean sold for fifty cents each.

I was not at all happy the next day to see this same man come through the door. He approached me and asked, "Can I speak with you?"

I remember thinking, *Oh, boy. What's the problem now?* Wondering if he wanted to register a complaint or request a refund, I grudgingly agreed.

As soon as we stepped into my dad's office, this fellow presented me with my dad's three-karat diamond ring. He told me that when he got home and examined one of the little tchotchke owls, he discovered my dad's ring. As he continued to share how he had already had it appraised for more than $3,000, I thought for sure we were about to play a version of "Let's Make a Deal."

I couldn't have been more wrong. This man who I had found so annoying explained his dad had a ring that was special to him, and he knew this ring would be special to me, so he wanted to return it. No bargaining. No haggling. Just a most unsolicited kindness.

"Cast your bread upon the water," Solomon teaches.

Some may choose to believe this abrasive man's unusual kindness had nothing to do with Jean slipping her special diamond ring into the offering plate decades before. I never will.

Our awesome God is faithful, but His timing is different than our timing.

# Faith Challenge Questions

- How have God's ways been different than your ways in your walk of faith?

- How has God's timing been different than yours in your journey with Jesus?

- How has God delivered you from shame?

- How have you misjudged someone?

# CHAPTER TWENTY-TWO:

# PASTORS ARE PEOPLE

*"Prayer, study, and suffering make a pastor."*
**Martin Luther**

One of the pearls of discovery that has surprised and impacted me most can be conveyed in this one cliche-sounding statement: "Pastors are people too."

To appreciate where I am coming from, it is helpful to note my grandfather, three of my uncles, and three of my cousins were all Lutheran pastors. You might say my family was "pastor-ized."

So, as I grew up, my frame of reference suggested a pastor was someone who went to four years of college followed by four years of seminary, was ordained, and then installed in a church of their denomination's choosing.

In my journey, I have discovered the perception most people have of clergy is formed when they are kids. The denomination or church affiliation within the family has a powerful influence on a person's outlook.

Looking back, it is no wonder Jean and I were led to an interdenominational Christian expression of faith. Jean's family was what one could describe as "non-practicing Catholic." Jean, her siblings, and friends all attended St. Patrick's Catholic School across the street from their Long Island City apartment. However, they rarely attended church.

I was baptized Lutheran, raised in the Episcopal church, attended a Catholic boarding school, have Methodist relatives, was led to Christ by a Baptist, and am now what most would describe as Pentecostal!

Before being born again, however, I walked away from all church-related stuff. When Jean and I were dating, we had many lively discussions about God. On date nights, we often drove through Jack-in-the-Box in Jackson Heights, Queens. We sat in our car, ate our tacos, and talked about Jean's best friend's mom, who was a "Charismatic Catholic" woman.

At the time, I was minoring in psychology at Brooklyn College and had strong opinions about these so-called born-again Christians. I was convinced these people who called themselves "born-again Christians" were simply weak, neurotic people who shouldn't be taken seriously. Furthermore, I thought Charismatic Christians who spoke in tongues were psychotic and in serious need of psychotropic medication!

God demonstrated His great sense of humor, allowing me to be born again two weeks before Jean was radically saved. Jean was always the voice in our wilderness, calling us to faith. I was the skeptic.

Over these past forty-plus years of walking with Jesus, we have witnessed many people come to faith. We have also observed how powerful a person's family traditions can be.

A person's identity as a Catholic, a Baptist, a Methodist, or some other denominational pedigree is usually rooted in their family traditions, customs, and convictions. If a person grows up as a Baptist, we often hear, "Well, by golly, my daddy was Baptist, my granddaddy was Baptist, and his daddy before him, was Baptist, so I'm a Baptist."

As someone who attended a Catholic boarding school, graduated from a Catholic High School, and married a Catholic girl, I can tell you, with full assurance, that this phenomenon is very real in Catholic families.

When a boy grows up in a Catholic family and feels "called to the ministry," there is only one ultimate goal, and that is to become a priest!

In addition to the rigorous academics, including four years of college and four years of seminary, Catholic priests make some serious vows, including vows of poverty and celibacy.

To illustrate a point, I want to share one of my all-time favorite jokes. However, before I do, I want to make it clear that I am not a "Catholic basher." Quite the opposite is true.

In our Higher Ground School of Ministry, we have a couple of classes on denominations. We remind our students: "If you love your Bible, thank a Catholic. God entrusted the Scriptures to them for a thousand years."

Furthermore, I am not mocking the vows of poverty or celibacy. I may not agree with them, but I do understand their scriptural genesis. It was a good Catholic, St. Augustine, who is credited for saying, "Unity in the essentials. Diversity in the non-essentials. Charity in all things." We try to live by that credo.

So, here's my joke.

Patrick was a terrific young man who grew up in a blue-collar Irish Catholic home in New York. He was bright, handsome, and very popular in school. Patrick was what many would describe as a lady's man. All the girls were crazy about him, and in turn, he was attracted to them. However, Patrick's dating came to a complete halt as he was finishing college. You see, Patrick was called to the ministry and was seriously contemplating becoming a priest.

After years of wrestling with the call, he decided he was "all in." Patrick completed his academics with excellence and made all of the vows required with his ordination, including the vow of poverty and the vow of celibacy.

Patrick was a great priest. He was as popular in his church as he had been in school. Everyone in his parish loved Father Patrick. However, only the Lord knew how hard it was for Patrick to honor his vow of celibacy. He really struggled in this area. Despite much consternation and a few minor setbacks, Father Patrick served faithfully in the priesthood for forty years.

In fact, the bishops were so impressed with his sterling tenure of service and sacrifice that they arranged for a special retirement package for Father Patrick in Rome, Italy.

His first-class accommodations included full access to the vast libraries within the Vatican itself. This was where the retired Father Patrick spent most of his time. He loved pouring over the old manuscripts, written mostly in his second language, Latin. After all, Father Patrick had become a Latin scholar and often taught Latin at the seminary level.

One cold winter morning, Patrick's friend and fellow retired priest, Father Luigi, went to the Vatican library to invite Patrick to join him for a cup of cappuccino. Father Luigi was agog when he discovered Patrick weeping over a particularly old manuscript he had discovered.

"What's wrong?" Father Luigi pleaded. "What are you reading that has caused you such anguish?"

Gasping for breath through painful sobs, Father Patrick looked up from his old Latin manuscript and, with tears in his eyes, cried, "We got it wrong. The word...the word is *celebrate!*"

Personally, I think this is a very funny joke. However, as is often the case with humor, there is a measure of truth lurking beneath the laughter.

In Scripture, the apostle Paul tells us it is better not to marry unless one burns with lust. So, to live celibate and be wholly committed to Christ is certainly a noble and lofty aspiration, but it's not for everyone.

As of 2008, more than 400,000 Catholic priests have been accused of sexual abuse. This outrageous stain on the church and the subsequent cover-up of these crimes has been abhorrent. More than 80 percent of the accused priests live in the United States.

According to Wikipedia, the average legal settlement for each case is between $300,000 to $400,000. This doesn't begin to take into account the devastation and lifelong trauma suffered by so many victims.

Could it be many of these priests were genuinely called to the ministry but not to celibacy?

We can read statistics like the ones mentioned here and shake our heads in shame. In my journey, I, unfortunately, caught a glimpse of this spiritual wreckage from a close-up.

As I've mentioned, in the mid-nineties, I served on ten consecutive *Kairos* prison weekends at Zephyrhills Correctional Institution. Several other pastors served on the team as well. One was a Catholic priest.

We prayed for many people in various situations during our team formation meetings, so it wasn't unusual to hear someone announce, "We need to pray for Father Bob." At first blush, I wrongly assumed Father Bob was dealing with a health challenge. As we discovered, his need for prayer ran much deeper than that.

You can imagine our chagrin when it was revealed our fellow clergy, Father Bob, was arrested for raping altar boys in his church. He was subsequently convicted and sentenced to many years in prison.

We have observed when a pastor falls, and it is usually because of one of the "three G's": gold, glory, or girls (or, in Father Bob's case, "guys").

During our many years of pastoring, Jean and I have witnessed the rise and fall of many men and women of God. Many have been pastors. Although most pastors don't crash and burn as dramatically as our Father Bob, It is helpful to remember pastors are just people. They aren't superhuman. They deal with the same health, family, financial, and situational challenges as everyone else.

Pastors are done a great disservice when people think otherwise. They are much better served to be put on a prayer list rather than up on a pedestal.

One of my best friends and mentors in ministry is Pastor John B. John served diligently and faithfully as a Methodist pastor for more than forty years. John and I served together (and survived many humiliating spiritual director skits) on several *Via de Cristo* weekends.

Preparing for their retirement, John and his dear wife, Crystal, purchased and renovated a beautiful home on a 3-acre lakeside property near their church.

A couple of years ago, on New Year's Day, John retired. His large church in Tavares, Florida, gave him and Crystal a grand retirement sendoff, complete with a brand-new golf cart to help them scoot around their new lakefront property. Eleven days later, John suffered an aortic aneurism and nearly died. Three surgeons worked on John for fourteen hours. They were so surprised he survived that they called him "Lazarus."

During his first three years of retirement, John suffered several minor strokes and survived heart valve replacement surgery. This medical marathon resulted in John living with brain damage. His compromised memory and cognitive skills haven't diminished his sense of humor one little bit.

Every month or so, I had the privilege of driving over to have brunch with my friend. John always gave me a tour of their beautiful vegetable garden, complete with a story or anecdote to brighten my day.

Although John spoke very softly because of damaged vocal cords, he always raved about what an angel his wife was and how their daughter, Amleset (who they adopted from Ethiopia), was thriving in school.

Last year John and Crystal sold their lakefront home and moved to a smaller home in Saint Petersburg. Amleset is excelling in college. John and Crystal live their life helping others as they can, one day at a time. Together, with grace and courage, they face John's serious ongoing medical issues.

*Pastor John Barham, Cole & me at an outreach in DeLand, FL.*

I mentioned three of my cousins were Lutheran ministers. I became good friends with one of them. My cousin, Henry, was the oldest of eight kids and a third-generation Lutheran pastor. After four years of college and four years of seminary, Henry was ordained and installed as associate pastor at a Lutheran church in Hickory, North Carolina. He and his wife served this congregation faithfully for ten years.

Henry's mother-in-law contracted cancer, so he, his wife, and their three beautiful sons moved to Sarasota, Florida, to help provide care. Henry was hired as associate pastor of the largest Lutheran church in Sarasota.

During Henry's fifth year serving as associate pastor, his wife ran off with their chiropractor and broke his heart. To add insult to injury, his church elected not to renew his contract, and he was out of a job. Instead of supporting Henry as his wife divorced him, his church abandoned him.

Henry was determined to stay in town, mainly so he could attend his son's soccer games. Initially, he took a job working the graveyard shift at a local 7-Eleven. There he sold beer to the same folks he used to serve communion to.

One special evening, during this season of great brokenness, Henry and I shared a close encounter with Christ on our uncle Ted's dock on Tampa Bay. Henry cried out to God, was born again, and baptized in the Holy Spirit.

Soon after this Road to Damascus awakening, a counseling position opened up for Henry. For the next several years, he attended all of his son's sporting events and helped people in recovery at Sarasota's First Step Recovery Center.

He eventually remarried and moved to Hendersonville, North Carolina, where he was hired as associate pastor of New Beginnings Assembly of God. Despite suffering a second divorce, Henry served his pastor and church with excellence for eighteen years.

Five days a week, Henry started his day with prayer and cleaning the church. He would then take the church van down the steep hill the church was situated on to the local Whole Food Market. Every weekday, this Whole Food Market donated thirty to forty boxes of the most delicious fruits and vegetables. After loading the van, Henry brought the haul back up the big hill to the church, where he would organize the bounty into scores of boxes. He then began his daily route of distributing these food boxes to scores of shut-ins. I am so very grateful to have had the great privilege of riding with Henry on one of his food runs. It took more than three hours just to deliver all of these designer fruits and vegetables.

For nine of his eighteen years as associate pastor, Henry carried out this heartfelt ministry to shut-ins with the steadfastness of a fascist railroad train.

One cold icy morning, February 23, 2015, as Henry was prepping the van for his food run, the van rolled over him and killed him. The officer who discovered Henry said that, apparently, Henry was trying to add brake fluid to the van, and it must have started to roll down the hill. He surmised Henry probably tried to stop the van from rolling, slipped on the ice, and fell under the rolling van. Henry was sixty-nine.

Although we were not able to attend Henry's celebration of life service, we were deeply touched to receive a beautiful card and a check for $500 to our ministry from Henry's third wife. She thanked us for our ministry to Henry. However, in many ways, it was Henry who ministered to us!

As I mentioned earlier, the pastor who married Jean and me in 1976 re-emerged in our life five years after we were married. Pastor Bill was a First Reformed pastor. Pastors in the First Reformed denomination also complete four years of college and four years of seminary before being ordained.

Pastor Bill was the one who sponsored Jean and me on our *Tres Días* weekend in 1982. Little did I know attending that one fateful interdenominational renewal weekend would be so formative.

Now, forty years later, I look back in mild shock and awe as I realize I have served on more than fifty *Tres Días*, *Via de Cristo*, and *Kairos* weekends. As I write this, I am scheduled to serve on another *Kairos* weekend in the fall.

As I "rewind the tape" in my mind, there are far too many God-incidences to share from so many weekends. The close encounters of the Jesus kind which unfold on these weekends make up a living tapestry of grace and graceful interactions between God and His kids.

However, our first weekend, *Tres Días* number ten in Huntington, Long Island, was revolutionary. The format of all of the *Via de Cristo* weekends centers around fifteen talks referred to as "*Rollos*." Ten of the *Rollos* are given by laypeople. Ten are given by the clergy.

As these rigorously honest and testimony-filled talks unfolded over the three-day weekend on *Tres Días* number ten, I slowly recognized all the clergy talks revealed something profound. These pastors all had something in common. They were all human.

Some of the pastors were divorced. Some were recovering alcoholics. Some battled depression, rejection, anger, and other challenges. Each one had a similar story of how our awesome loving God turned their mess into a message.

At some point during this grace-filled weekend, a seed was planted deep in my soul. A question was forming in my heart. "If God could use these men as pastors, could He use me?" If so, how? I had never even completed college.

Over the coming months and years, as Jean and I served on *Via de Cristo* weekends and in our local church, our call to full-time ministry grew stronger and stronger.

After moving to Florida in 1985, while I was working full-time at WEDU TV, Jean and I were blessed to serve for a couple of years as children's ministers at a small church in Tampa. Jesus and the kids stole our hearts.

The next church we attended had a ministry school. We completed their training and received a ministry license. Soon after being licensed, we were invited to serve as associate pastors at a large inner-city Assembly of God church in Tampa.

I continued to work full-time at WEDU TV during the three years Jean and I served at Freedom Ministries Assembly of God. We look back upon those years and laughingly say, "If we weren't called, that would have cured us."

Fast forward to more than twenty-plus years, and we can't even count the number of men and women we have known who were at one time on-fire full-time pastors and are no longer in the ministry. I am sharing this observation simply to illuminate the fact pastoring is a tough job.

Over my many years on this earth, I have had many different jobs. While attending Brooklyn College, I drove a Yellow Cab in Manhattan. After a twelve-hour shift of driving a cab, your entire body seems to vibrate for a while after you get out of the cab.

As a young man, I also worked at 84 Lumber. After a long day of unloading trucks, I could really feel the day's exercise in my back.

For years I worked as a waiter at Oggi's Restaurant in Manhattan. My feet would hurt after a long shift.

In my early twenties, I was employed as a karate instructor at Tracy's Karate Studios in Forest Hills, New York. After a full day in the dojo, my fingers would often hurt after getting them jammed from blocking kicks.

For a score of years working in broadcasting sales and management, the stress of hitting the next performance goals often left me mentally exhausted.

Like so many things in life, unless someone has walked where you have walked, they can't fully understand the challenges involved in carrying out certain responsibilities. Serving as a pastor places a demand on your entire spirit, soul, and body. There is spiritual warfare involved in everyday activities. From this reality, there are no days off. The devil is real. He seeks to steal, kill and destroy every pastor who is living for the Lord. The redeeming truth is, for those who are truly called, God manifests His grace and empowers the minister to war from a place of victory.

Yes, pastoring is and should always be a calling. However, it is a job. Pastoring is a function, not an identity. The blessings of praying with people as they receive or rededicate their life to Christ certainly outweigh the challenges of calling prodigals home or comforting the grief-stricken at a loved one's deathbed.

However, along with the praying and the preaching, the baptisms and the funerals, along with the joy and jubilation of worshipping with the saints, there is often a shroud of loneliness and discouragement only those who have walked there truly understand.

Yes, pastors are people too.

If you are fortunate enough to have a pastor who loves the Lord and is doing his utmost to serve and glorify God, pray for them. Pray about asking where you can serve or how you can help.

## Faith Challenge Questions

- Have you ever had a personal relationship with a full-time pastor?

- How often do you pray for your pastor?

- How has a pastor encouraged or helped you?

- How do you serve in your local church?

# A Pearl of Healing

## A Valliant Soldier with Leprosy

*"There is a river whose streams make glad the city of God" (Psalm 46:4).*

In 2 Kings chapter 5, we read about an army commander by the name of Naaman. The Scriptures tell us that Naaman was "a valiant man, but he had leprosy." He came to Elisha for help, but he didn't like Elisha's prescription to "dip in the Jordan seven times." Naaman was so furious that he left in a huff. No doubt that was so simple it sounded silly—probably like "go jump in a lake" would sound to us today. Naaman angrily said: "Aren't the rivers of Damascus better than these waters of Israel?"

I understand where Naaman was coming from. I was baptized in the Jordan River, and it really is nothing to look at. Naaman almost missed his healing! After some persistence on the part of his servant, though, Naaman agreed and dipped himself in the Jordan. He was made whole again.

Leprosy was such a diabolical disease not because it caused much pain but because it caused a loss of all sensation in the afflicted areas. The deadened areas made the individual vulnerable to serious injury without even being aware of it. Today I believe America is suffering from an epidemic of leprosy: spiritual leprosy. We have become deadened and hardened to the things of God. We are a great nation, but we have leprosy! Our country is in real danger: not from the Taliban, but from ourselves! Our legislators are taking "under God" out of the Pledge of Allegiance, prayer out of schools, the ten commandments out of our court-houses, and our religious leaders are promoting gay marriage and protecting pedophile priests.

What's the answer? I believe the solution is so simple that it sounds silly: we must turn back to God! Christians must emulate Naaman's servant and persist in proclaiming the only real solution: "But seek first his kingdom and his righteousness, and all these things will be given to you as well" (Matthew 6:33). Psalm 46:4 says: "There is a river whose streams make glad the city of God." We must get under the spout where the glory pours out! We must prioritize His presence and spend quality time in worship and His Word. Don't wait for a church service. Get alone with the Lord in your car. Pop in some anointed Christian music and sing out loud to the Lord. Don't worry about what the guy at the red light is going to think! What does that matter? (He probably thinks you're crazy anyway.) By the time you're singing the seventh song on the CD, remember Naaman and how he found healing as he dipped himself seven times in the River Jordan! Oh, jump! Jump! Jump in the river!

# CHAPTER TWENTY-THREE:

# SPIRIT-FORMED

*"The church is the gym of the soul."*

**Sylvester Stallone**

As I have mentioned several times in different ways, *A Shepherd's Pearls* is a vehicle through which I hope to convey truths, insights, and "aha moments" that have come through many years of discovery.

In our Higher Ground School of Ministry, we say: "God can't steer a parked car." Of course, God can do whatever He wants. After all, two of the greatest discoveries anyone can make are:

1. There is a God.

2. I am not Him!

So, perhaps it is better to say, "God will not steer a parked car!" The point is we learn as we go. As we press on in our quest to go where the Lord says, *"Go,"* and do what the Lord says, "*Do*," we grow as we go.

These discoveries are both old and new. When God brings revelation to our soul, unlike manna in the wilderness, it remains eternally fresh and new.

The wonderful way the Lord unfolds our calling is much like kicking out a carpet. He often reveals just the next step or two. We walk out the Spirit's promptings and instructions by faith and then discover the next unfolding of His will.

As we look back, we see His plan with brilliant clarity. We can see God's fingerprints on different times and seasons in our journey. Truly, He is the Potter, and we are the clay. He is diligent in shaping us and forming us, and breaking us when necessary.

We also see the places where we have missed it, and we all do. Only Jesus carried out the Father's will without a misstep. The rest of us are, in a sense, stumbling to glory.

As we recognize God's handiwork in our life, our faith is strengthened. Like David, who recalled conquering the lion and the bear before facing Goliath, we are given the tools, times, and experiences to prepare us for the next challenge.

If someone asked me what the difference is between being Spirit-born, Spirit-filled, and Spirit-formed, I would answer, "About twenty years."

Please let me explain. As I shared, I was raised in the church and almost missed heaven by eighteen inches, the distance between my head and my heart. Sure, I knew what we were celebrating at Christmas and Easter, but my understanding was just in my head and not in my heart.

It was not until the Lord brought a wonderful, funny, bold non-religious Baptist brother into my life that I was challenged by Jesus' exhortation, "You must be born again."

Before Tim led me to Jesus at 2 p.m. on January 21, 1979, I would look you straight in the eye and tell you with all sincerity that I was a Christian. I wasn't a Jew or a Muslim. I had been baptized as a baby. I was confirmed in the church. Yet, like ripe fruit ready to fall from the tree, my heart was strangely mesmerized and puzzled by this charge to "be born again."

I remember going to one of my three Lutheran pastor uncles and asking, "Uncle Corley, what do you think about these born-again Christians?"

His answer only kicked my questioning heart into another gear, "Jim, that's the only kind of Christians there are."

Within weeks, I found myself accepting my sales manager's offer to pray for me. Tim happened to have a key to a big Baptist church in Rocky Mount, North Carolina, where we worked. Little did I know, as Tim was unlocking the church door, the Lord was about to unlock the door to my stubborn heart.

As Tim began to pray and lift my needs to the Lord, the blessed Holy Spirit gently and powerfully descended on me like a thick warm blanket. The only words I spoke were, "God, if You're there, please help me." Looking back, in some ways, it feels like this encounter took place five minutes ago. In another way, it feels like this Road to Damascus awakening happened a lifetime ago. It was, for me, a defining moment.

As if it happened yesterday, I remember walking from that church and hearing the birds sing as if for the first time. As I looked up at the sky, it seemed bluer than blue. When I got home, Jean wept with joy before I spoke even one word. I was, without question, discussion, or explanation, a new creation in Christ. The old was gone. The new had come.

This discovery came after twenty-five years of living life on my terms. Proverbs 14:12 warns us, "There is a way that appears to be right, but in the end it leads to death." So it was with me.

So, it is with every person on this planet who is not born again. Jesus wasn't kidding when He said we "must be born again." It matters not if this Spirit birth takes place with the fireworks of a Road to Damascus conversion or with the peaceful assurance the Ethiopian eunuch found with Philip in Acts 8:36 when he exclaimed, "Here is water. What can stand in the way of my being baptized?"

Some call it "getting saved" or "being born again." Some reference the new birth as being "converted" or "redeemed." Regardless of the label with which we describe it, the most important thing is we are Spirit-born.

Regardless of how we come to our awakening, it is

eternally essential we come to "know-in-our-knower" we are His. First John 3:1 celebrates this grace by saying, "See what great love the Father has lavished on us, that we should be called children of God! And that is what we are."

One of the immediate irrefutable pieces of evidence to my own heart that I was Spirit-born was a new insatiable hunger to read the Bible. Not only was I hungry to read the Bible, but for the first time in my life, the Scriptures made sense. Jesus walked up and down the pages with me as I poured through the Gospels, Acts, and Corinthians.

Within the first six months of this newfound zeal, I started drinking beer again. Up until this point in my life, drinking beer hadn't been a problem. It soon became a problem. One beer was becoming too many, and twelve weren't enough. The great paradox in my experience was my increasing thirst for beer didn't diminish my hunger for God's Word. I had many a Bible study with a cold six-pack of Heinekens!

Without intending to, I found myself in what I now describe as a "Romans Chapter 7" existence. The thing I hated (getting drunk) I kept on doing, and the thing I wanted to do (honor the Lord and my family) I couldn't find the power to do.

As I was growing in my Scripture study and alcohol dependence, I stumbled across I Corinthians chapter 12. This passage of Scripture contains Paul's explanation of the gifts of the Holy Spirit.

I brought my questions about the gifts of the Spirit to

the good man who led me to Jesus.

"Tim, what is Paul talking about here in 1 Corinthians 12?" I inquired with childlike curiosity. "What is this gift of speaking in tongues? Is this available to us today?" I queried.

Tim explained, "These gifts went out when the apostles died. They didn't have the canon of Scripture, so God gave them those gifts."

"Oh, okay," I ignorantly accepted.

Fast forward past countless hangovers and AA meetings, and you will find me continuing to stumble around in my "Romans Chapter 7" valley of despair.

I was memorizing Scripture, praying without ceasing, living one day at a time for thirty days or so, and then falling to the drink. Oh, wretched man was I. Who would deliver me from this death?

All the while, Jean and I were attending an Assembly of God church. At Bellrose Assembly, they spoke of being a Spirit-filled Christian.

Here I was, a born-again alcoholic who didn't fit in the church or AA. Certainly, there must be an answer to my dilemma, but where?

For a full year, I earnestly prayed about this business of being "baptized in the Holy Spirit." Every night before going to sleep, I prayed, "Lord, if this baptism of the Holy Spirit is from You, I want it. If it's not from You, please keep it from me."

I shared earlier how while working as a waiter at Oggi's Restaurant in Manhattan, this prayer was answered.

As I was alone one day, setting up the restaurant, the Holy Spirit invaded my simple songs of praise with an unmistakable *kabod* presence. I found myself singing silly syllables which made no earthly sense. Yet, the marrow of my bones resonated with a knowing-in-my-knower that *this* was my personal Pentecost!

Yes, my friend, no matter what the cost, we need a Pentecost! We need a personal Pentecost.

Through this discovery, Acts 1:8 took on new meaning. There Jesus tells us, "You will receive power when the Holy Spirit comes on you; and you will be my witnesses."

The *dunamis* dynamite power that flooded my soul at Oggi's Restaurant on that blessed day was another defining moment in my journey with Jesus.

As I share in my book—*Step 13: Do You Want to Get Well?*—this infilling of the Holy Spirit broke every chain alcohol had on me. I discovered the new wine is better than the old. The truth is, I never stopped drinking. I just changed my drink! As a result, my walk began to line up with my talk. My marriage was on the mend. Our bills were being paid. Shame was diminishing. Joy was increasing. His call began to be revealed in our life.

Much in the same way as on the day I was born again, I mistook this infilling of the Holy Spirit as a type of finish line when, in fact, it was another starting gun.

When I was born again, there was such a great "aha

moment," it felt as if my life was changed forever and I had, in a sense, arrived.

It was true that my life was forever changed on January 21, 1979. The scales had fallen from my eyes, and I would never be the same. However, just as a newborn baby needs milk and time and a lot of help before it can feed itself or learn how to walk, so are we when we are born again. This is an easy discovery all born-again Christians realize sooner or later.

It is perhaps not as obvious to recognize there is a big difference between being Spirit-filled and becoming Spirit-formed.

On the day I was baptized in the Holy Spirit, it felt like "the aha moment of all aha moments." Chains were broken. I was free. I had tapped into a new power for living.

After being filled with the Holy Spirit, I discovered my prayer language was a new weapon. A new door was unlocked to greater intimacy. I was able to walk in Jude 1:20, "building yourselves up in your most holy faith and praying in the Holy Spirit."

Paul describes our prayer language beautifully in Romans 8:26, "We do not know what we ought to pray for, but the Spirit himself intercedes for us through wordless groans."

It took me years to discover that there are many fillings of the Holy Spirit. Walking into the baptism of the Holy Spirit is not a "one and done" encounter. It is a new encounter but not a destination or super-spiritual qualification.

In his book, *The Three Battlegrounds*, Francis Frangipane says, "Victory begins with the name of Jesus on our lips. It is consummated by the nature of Jesus in our hearts."

There are many who confess Jesus with their lips but deny Him with their lifestyle.

It is sobering to discover many self-described "Spirit-filled Christians" are, indeed, filled with the spirit, but not the Holy Spirit!

Now, don't get me wrong. I understand if someone is walking around with a hammer, everything may begin to look like a nail. I'm not talking about fault-finding or being judgmental.

In Matthew 7:16, Jesus said, "By their fruit you will recognize them." As we journey with Jesus for a while, we recognize all that glitters is not gold.

Regardless of what label or title a Christian may wear, we are all capable of being filled with spirits of pride, lust, fear, religion, confusion, bitterness, or a dozen other spirits that are not the Holy Spirit. For all of us, being yielded to the Holy Spirit is a daily choice. It's humbling to realize Christians are capable of any sin under the sun except the sin of unbelief.

When I was ten years old, my dad gave me a big, beautiful Wilson baseball glove for my birthday. To help me break it in, he poured some 3-IN-ONE oil on the pocket of the glove, put a baseball in the glove, and wrapped a big rubber band around it. He then tucked it under my mattress, so I could sleep on it overnight.

As you might imagine, the next morning, the well-oiled glove was still stiff and new. The only way to break it in was to use it repeatedly. Eventually, that glove was broken in and served me very well as the first baseman on my little league team.

In the same way, becoming a Spirit-formed Christian requires a lot more than one good outpouring of oil. It takes years of being used over and over again.

Years ago, after my wife and I were hurt by someone in the church who betrayed us, I prayed, "Lord, how do we learn to genuinely bless those who persecute us?"

His one-word reply continues to echo in my soul. He simply said, "Practice."

Hebrews 5:14 tells us, "But solid food is for the mature, who by constant use have trained themselves to distinguish good from evil."

Furthermore, it is a lifelong process. Paul promises in Philippians 1:6, "He who began a good work in you will carry it on to completion." We are all being processed. There is always higher ground in God.

John the Beloved promises in 1 John 3:2, "Dear friends, now we are children of God, and what we will be has not yet been made known. But we know that when Christ appears, we shall be like him, for we shall see him as he is."

Earlier in the same epistle, John speaks to three distinct groups of Christians: children, strong young men, and fathers. One group is not more Christian than the other. They are simply at a different place in their journey.

We continue in our journey with Jesus as we answer His call to maturity. We press on into adulthood in Christ by the same spirit with which we came to Christ in the first place, namely, by grace.

Regardless of where we are in our journey or calling, we all have one call in common. The Lord revealed this common denominator to me in a picture one day as I was in prayer.

In my mind's eye, I saw a man reaching up with one hand and reaching down with his other hand. With one hand, he was taking hold of someone's hand who was higher than he. With the other hand, he was reaching down to lift someone who was in a lower place.

Dr. Jack Hayford has impacted my life over the years. He is a true father in the faith who has authored more than fifty books and nearly 600 hymns. Dr. Hayford is someone I look up to as one who is further down the road of Christian maturity than me.

Jack Hayford is a brilliant pastor and teacher. He is a chancellor of a seminary and, for many years, has been a powerful voice on radio and television all over the world. Perhaps what distinguishes Dr. Hayford most is his genuine spirit of humility. Although he is unashamedly charismatic in his theology, he consistently delivers the full gospel message with a disarming measure of love and grace.

In his book, *Living the Spirit-Formed Life*, Jack Hayford says, "Just as grace is the means by which we receive salvation, grace is the means for letting God work in His might and power for our lifelong walk with Him."

With our Higher Ground School of Ministry, we have had the privilege of working with many ministers in training over many years. We often recognize God's fingerprints on our ministry students as they share how God is working with them.

It is a sign of a close walk with the Lord when a believer shares how God is dealing with them about this area or that. The Holy Spirit is often gentle in His corrections and tweaking, but He is diligent in teaching us and helping us mature.

You've probably heard the expression, "The Holy Spirit is a gentleman." I would submit to you that nothing could be further from the truth. Yes, gentleness is a fruit of the Spirit, and God often works with us in a most loving and gentle way. However, He is no gentleman. The truth is He's not a man at all. He is God, and He will do what He wills, how He wills, when He wills, and the way He wills without apology or explanation. Just ask Saul of Tarsus or Ananias and Sapphira!

One definition of the Greek word metamorphosis is: "the transformation from an immature form to an adult form." Such transformation takes time.

Most of us have heard many messages on "working out our salvation." Many preachers will reference Philippians 2:12, where Paul exhorts us to "work out [our] salvation with fear and trembling." I am so grateful there is no period at the end of that verse!

Praise God, Paul goes on to say, "For it is God who works in you both to will and to do His good pleasure."

We are like that baseball glove I received on my tenth birthday. God is working with us and within us to help form us into a pliable, Spirit-formed son or daughter. So, how do we press on to our destiny of becoming mature Spirit-formed believers? I believe the answer to that question is the same answer a man on a New York subway received when he asked a fellow passenger, "Hey, buddy, how do I get to Carnegie Hall from here?"

The man looked up from reading his morning paper and said, "Practice, brother. Practice!"

How do we press on in our call to become Spirit-formed? "Practice, brother. Practice!"

## Faith Challenge Questions

- When were you born again?

- How has Jesus changed your life?

- Have you been baptized in the Holy Spirit?

- Who do you reach up to in the Lord?

- Who have you reached out to help them grow in the Lord?

# CHAPTER TWENTY-FOUR:

# JOY

*"You don't choose your family. They are God's gift
to you, as you are to them."*

**Desmond Tutu**

Of all the discoveries we make in our journey, finding joy is among the greatest. The Scriptures teach the joy of the Lord is our strength. A Christian without joy is like Samson with a bad haircut!

Jesus said one of the reasons He came is so we could have joy and have it to the full. Joy is a birthright of every Spirit-born child of God.

After Jesus sent out the disciples, they returned with many great testimonies of the powerful works they performed in the Lord's name. He responded to their exuberance by encouraging them to rejoice because their names were written in the Lamb's book of life. So it is with us. Regardless of what accomplishments, breakthroughs, or revelations we may encounter, there is no greater wellspring of joy than "knowing-in-our-knower" that our sins are forgiven and that our citizenship is in heaven.

However, the challenges and cares of this world can rob us of our joy. We all have good days and bad days. So, where do we turn when we go through those times when we, like David in Psalm 51:12, find ourselves praying for God to "restore to me the joy of your salvation"?

Certainly, we pray. James 5:13 exhorts us, "Is anyone among you in trouble? Let them pray." Let's face it; if we lose our joy, we are in trouble. Without joy, our sense of purpose is obscured, and our day-to-day activities become drudgery.

Isaiah 61:3 speaks of God giving us a "garment of praise instead of a spirit of despair." There is no question that prayer and praise are mighty weapons in God's arsenal. The Word of God is also essential in receiving a fresh infusion of joy. When we turn to the Scriptures and review God's many promises, we are renewed. In Ephesians 6:17, Paul describes the full armor of God. The only offensive weapon Paul mentions is "the sword of the Spirit, which is the word of God." The writer of Hebrews reminds us in Hebrews 4:12, "For the word of God is alive and active. Sharper than any double-edged sword."

We who have been walking this walk with Jesus for a while come to realize there is an added power in speaking the Word of God out loud. In Genesis, we see God speak to the darkness and say, "Light be." Declaration brings manifestation.

Instead of speaking to God about how big our problems are, we learn to speak to our problems and declare how big our God is!

Prayer and praise and declaring God's Word out loud should be as natural to us believers as walking and breathing.

God has graced all of us with another joy bringer that is often hidden in plain sight. It is all around us. It is an essential part of God's design and one of God's most amazing graces. Yet, we often take this gift for granted. I am referring to the gift of family. In 3 John 1:4, John the Beloved says, "I have no greater joy than to hear my children are walking in the truth."

This is certainly true in my life. As a matter of fact, I could simply say, "I have no greater joy than my children." The fact that they are walking in the truth is icing on the cake. Having our kids serve with us as pastors in the same church for more than twenty years is exceedingly, abundantly more than I could have asked or imagined. This joy becomes sweeter with each passing year.

If we are not mindful, the busyness and many distractions of this world can eclipse the joy God intends to bring us through our family.

Allowing a misunderstanding or offense to go unresolved can also rob us. I know this firsthand. I shared earlier how I left my dad when I was seventeen and didn't speak to him for seven years.

In my case, God turned lemons into lemonade. God brought a beautiful restoration to my dad and me. When God restores, He doesn't just bring that which is restored back to its original condition. He brings it back better than before. So He did with Dad and me.

Along with my relationship with my dad being fully restored and blessed, God gave me a deep appreciation for the importance of communicating with our kids once I became a father. Throughout our kids growing up and especially when our children were in their teen years, God tempered my fathering with a constant awareness that relationships are not indestructible. In many ways, because Jean and I were so young and immature when we became parents, we grew up with our kids.

Having spent more than half of our forty-plus years walking with Jesus in full-time ministry, you can imagine how many broken and dysfunctional families we have encountered. You may be reading this and thinking, *My upbringing and family have been anything but a source of joy.*

Our church family was recently made aware of a situation where a precious young girl was repeatedly raped by her stepfather for years. The stepfather is now in prison, and the young lady is facing a mountainous journey of inner healing in the wake of this kind of abuse.

We certainly understand the pains of divorce. It is sobering to note approximately half of the marriages end up in divorce. It's even more humbling to recognize the divorce rate "in the church" is not much different than the divorce rate among the unchurched.

In light of all the abuse, divorce, and dysfunction so prevalent in so many families, how can I suggest family is a source of joy? I'm glad you asked.

We have a dear friend who killed five people while driving drunk about thirty years ago. The twenty-seven years, 111 days he spent in prison as a result is just a small portion of the pain and punishment caused by this one tragic accident.

Was the automobile to blame? Absolutely not. The automobile manufacturers design cars to carry out good purposes. In the same way, God has designed the family to be a vehicle for good. It is man's stubborn propensity to pride, selfishness, and sin which often cause the gift of family to crash.

God's design for family is at the bedrock of His creation. Adam was alone, and God saw this wasn't good. So, God created Eve. This was the real "first family."

God's celebration of family is clearly seen throughout Scripture. Long before Ancestry.com, God was working through the generations to accomplish His purposes.

We celebrate "the God of Abraham, Isaac, and Jacob." Beyond those three generations of God's chosen, we see God's fingerprints on the twelve tribes (families) of Israel and beyond.

Moses was blessed and helped by his father-in-law, Jethro, as well as his sister Miriam. King David, who gave us most of the book of Psalms, fathered Solomon, who gave us most of the book of Proverbs.

As one peruses the families and family lines highlighted in the Old Testament, it is fascinating to note that Jesus came through the line of Leah and Bathsheba! As James (the half-brother of Jesus) would later reveal, "mercy triumphs over judgment"!

Yes, Abraham had his Ishmael, but he also fathered Isaac. David had his Absalom, but He also fathered Solomon. God's grace is bigger than man's sin. It always was. It will always be.

Perhaps the greatest scriptural evidence of God's love and design for family is witnessed through the miracle of Christmas. God could have certainly sent His Son to us with an army of angels on fiery chariots with trumpets in their hands. Yet, He chose to bring the Savior of the world to us through His gift of family.

Peter the Rock was brought to Jesus by his brother Andrew. James and John, the Sons of Thunder, were brothers, as were the disciples Jude and James the Lesser (meaning shorter or younger). Jesus was baptized by His cousin John. Paul encouraged his spiritual son, Timothy, by mentioning the faithfulness of Timothy's grandmother, Lois.

The crown of God's design for man is revealed to us through God's only begotten Son. He could have sent a lawyer or a scientist or a business tycoon. He sent His Son.

In Galatians 4, we are reminded we are God's children.

We are blessed to recognize God sent His Spirit into our hearts, and our hearts cry, "Abba! Father!" He is our Daddy. We are His family.

Jean and I recently had the great joy of dedicating our great-granddaughter, Everly Rose, to the Lord. Jean's eighty-eight-year young mom participated in our church service. We stood before the Lord with five generations being represented. God's faithfulness was on display for all the world to see.

The psalmist said, "Things we have heard and known, things our ancestors have told us. We will not hide them from their descendants; we will tell the next generation the praiseworthy deeds of the Lord" (Psalm 78:3).

As we look across the generations, we can see the handiwork and fingerprints of God.

Every month when I was a kid, I would receive a new issue of Highlights Magazine. Each issue always had one of those drawings with a dozen or so items cleverly hidden in plain sight and a list of the items you had to find. That was my favorite.

Many issues of my Highlight Magazines also had one of those "connect the dots" puzzles. This was a blank page with numbered dots in what appeared, at first, to be in random order. As you followed the instructions and connected the dots by number, a picture would appear.

In a similar way, both in Scripture and in our daily life, as we connect the dots throughout family lines, we can often see the face of Christ appear. Some of God's greatest blessings are often hidden in plain sight. God is faithful, and He works through the generations.

I shared earlier how my family grew up admiring America's pastor, Billy Graham. Rev. Graham greatly impacted me long before I ever knew we would have the joy of meeting him one day. Incredibly, I had the great privilege of working for him and his son, Franklin, as their Florida director for the Billy Graham Evangelistic Association for three years. During those years, my love and appreciation for Dr. Graham and his family only grew. Learning about Billy and Ruth, their parents, kids, and grandkids was like connecting the dots in one of those Highlight Magazines.

With every book I read and every story I heard from Billy's kids and grandkids, the face of Christ became clearer and clearer. Are they a perfect family? They would be the very first to tell you, "Absolutely not." Perhaps therein lies the great lesson I am trying to point to. Our perfect God works perfectly through real people and imperfect families, especially if they will stay connected.

*Jean, Gigi & me*

Jean and I still laugh about the first time we had the pleasure of having ice cream with Billy's first daughter, Gigi. On the way to the ice cream shop, Jean and I told each other, "Let's not go in there and talk about Billy Graham. Everyone that meets Gigi probably just wants to talk to her about her famous dad."

The reason we laugh is we weren't with Gigi more than five minutes before *she* was talking about her daddy! She was obviously a daddy's girl, and her love and admiration for her daddy only deepened our affection. Gigi has since become a friend. She is graced with the same down-to-earth, unpretentious spirit we loved in her dad.

In one of the first chapters of *A Shepherd's Pearls*, I referenced the apostle Paul's admonition that "in Christ we may have ten thousand counselors but few fathers in the faith." I went on to suggest those counselors of which Paul speaks may include books we read and people we encounter on our journey.

For me, the Graham family has been a source of inspiration, and I would be remiss if I didn't point you to a few pearls which I have discovered in my journey. I pray you will earmark this page and go back and order some of the following books which have greatly blessed Jean and me:

- *How To Be Born Again* by Billy Graham.
- *It's My Turn* by Ruth Bell Graham.
- *Currents of the Heart* by Gigi Graham.
- *Jesus in Me* by Anne Graham Lotz.
- *Forgiving My Father, Forgiving Myself* by Ruth Graham.
- *Rebel With a Cause* by Franklin Graham.
- *One Way Love* by Tullian Tchividjian.
- *Redeemed* by Will Graham.
- *A Foreign Devil in China* by John Pollock.

Along with preaching to more people in person than anyone in history, Billy Graham wrote thirty-three books over seventy years. His wife, Ruth, wrote six books. Billy and Ruth's kids and grandkids have together written more than one hundred books.

My favorite is *A Foreign Devil in China: The Story of Dr. L. Nelson Bell*. It is special not only because it was personally given to me by Billy's daughter, Gigi, but also because it reads like an adventure thriller.

Dr. Bell and his wife, Virginia, were Ruth Bell Graham's parents. Dr. Bell was an amazing Christian man. He was a brilliant surgeon who, along with his fearless and godly wife, served tirelessly and courageously on the front lines in war-torn China for twenty-five years. This is where Ruth was born and lived as a child.

After growing up and marrying, Billy and Ruth Graham lived in Dr. Nelson and Virginia Bell's home, where they were mentored long before they became famous. I found it fascinating to go behind the scenes and learn some of the rest of the story, as Paul Harvey used to say.

If you accept the challenge and tap into the above list of suggested readings, you will see the face of Christ appear as you connect the dots. It may take a little longer than connecting the dots in a Highlights Magazine, but you will indeed be blessed to see the handiwork of God.

You may be thinking, *Well, this is well and good for families like the Grahams, but what does this have to do with my family and me?* I'm glad you asked!

God's gift of family is intended to be a source of joy and purpose and identity. If this is not being actualized in your day-to-day journey, I would suggest sin is to blame. Maybe it is your sin or someone else's, but sin (missing the mark) is probably to blame.

*Jean & I meeting Rev. Billy Graham*

Sin will make you stupid. Sin hurts people. Hurt people hurt people. If you are not able to see God's handiwork as you look at your family, past, and present, it is most likely because someone's sin caused a disconnect. Hurt, bitterness, and unforgiveness can blind our eyes to God's blessings which, as I said, are often hidden in plain sight.

If you have been hurt or offended by someone in your family, forgive. As Christians, we are blessed to be forgiven and called to be forgiving. This is, as we say in recovery programs, "simple but not easy."

Certainly, there are family situations and circumstances that are beyond our repair. However, our experience in ministry has revealed most family challenges can be healed through the simple, profound miracle of forgiveness.

Some of the strongest families we know have experienced a disconnect along the way. Yet, through the grace of forgiveness were reconnected and grew closer than ever.

Did you know when someone breaks an arm or leg and goes through the casting and healing process, their limb comes through the ordeal even stronger than before? Families restored by the grace and mercy of God are like this. It is never too late to call upon the Lord to reconnect those fractured family relationships.

We can't control what was done to us, but each of us is 100 percent responsible for how we respond. When we respond with grace and forgiveness, we are the ones who are blessed. We are washed and cleansed and healed of the bitterness and bitter root judgments which can rob us of the joy found in one of God's greatest graces, namely our family.

Having been at the deathbed of many people over the years, I can tell you with full assurance that when it all is said and done, at the end of the day, we won't be looking for our bank book or academic accolades to comfort us. We want our family.

Don't wait until your deathbed to pick up the telephone and call your loved ones. Do it today. You may just uncork a well of joy and laughter that is waiting for you.

Realign yourself with God's plan for your best life. Reacquaint yourself with your family.

# Faith Challenge Questions

- What brings you joy?

- When were you most joyful?

- When have you lost your joy?

- How important is your family to you?

- Who in your family do you need to call?

# A Pearl of New Birth

## The Family of God

*"See what great love the Father has lavished on us"*
*(1 John 3:1).*

I am part of the family of God. I have been born again! I'm saved by grace, empowered by joy, inspired by love, protected by angels, and established in His Word.

There's a song in my heart, a bounce in my step, a light in my eyes, and His name is always on my lips. I'm no longer ashamed, alone, afraid, or abandoned. God is my Father, Jesus my brother, and my guide is none other than the stone-rolling, death-defying, awe-inspiring Spirit of the living God!

I am a part of the family of God. I have a place set at the Master's table. But before my Father calls me home, to sit at the table with all the saints…He has work here for me—that must be done. There's a race here for me—that must be run. And battles right here—that must be won.

So, I'll work like there's no tomorrow, dance like nobody's watching, and run with the fire of God.

I'm a giver, not a taker; a doer, not a faker. I'll walk the walk and talk the talk, for I am a part of the family of God. I will not flee, fear, fail, or falter, but with faith, I'll fight the fight.

I am a part of the family of God! I have been born again!

# CHAPTER TWENTY-FIVE:

# WORDS

*"Words have a magical power. They can bring either the greatest happiness or the deepest despair."*

**Sigmund Freud**

The story goes about a little five-year-old boy who was suffering through a long Sunday sermon at church. When the long-winded preacher said, "And in conclusion..." the little boy leaned into his dad and asked, "Dad, what does 'in conclusion' mean?"

The father smiled and said, "Nothing, son. It means absolutely nothing!"

As I began writing *A Shepherd's Pearls*, I shared with you how I felt compelled by the Lord to share some of the pearls of discovery we have made in our forty-five years of marriage and forty-plus years of walking with Jesus.

"And in conclusion," it is my sincere heartfelt prayer that some of these discoveries and ramblings have encouraged you in your journey with Jesus.

Paul tells us in Romans 1:11–12, "I long to see you so that I may impart to you some spiritual gift to make you strong—that is, that you and I may be mutually encouraged by each other's faith."

God is faithful; He always sends a "Barnabas" (son of encouragement) when we need one. I pray I have been "a Barnabas" to you. I pray the spirit of encouragement will infuse your soul and strengthen you for your journey ahead. The best is yet to come!

Paul tells us in 2 Corinthians 4:7, "We have this treasure in jars of clay." The truth is we all, like clay pots, are created to contain. It is also true that we all leak. Praise God; He has created us to be refillable!

Now, what or who we fill ourselves with shapes our world and greatly impacts our family, friends, and all those we encounter on a day-to-day basis.

The importance of Ephesians 5:18 can't be overstated: "Be filled with the Spirit."

What we allow into our ear gates and eye gates determines, in large part, what we are filled with.

As I begin to "circle the airport," I am compelled to point to one more pearl of great price, namely words.

Words matter. Words are important. Words forecast our future. We will, eventually, have what we say.

The intimate relationship between our words and the condition of our hearts is irrefutable.

In Matthew 12:34, Jesus says, "For the mouth speaks what the heart is full of."

I submit to you the words we choose to speak will either cultivate or corrupt the spiritual health of our own hearts.

After twenty years of studying the brain, the brilliant scientist, Dr. Caroline Leaf, teaches that "our mind has dominion over our brain." In plain English, we are not robots. We are responsible for the words we speak and the influence they have on others. We are all works in progress. Everyone, from time to time, says things they shouldn't say and doesn't say things they should. Progress, not perfection, is of paramount importance in our journey.

As Dr. Harbuck from Omega Seminary says, "Without accountability, there is no responsibility." Now, we must recognize no one "holds us accountable" without our permission. We hold ourselves accountable to whomever we choose. It is an act of our free will.

It certainly didn't happen overnight, but over time, Jean and I grew to hold ourselves accountable to each other for the things we say. This has been a great help to us in our life and ministry.

When one of us begins to sag in our enthusiasm or positivity and a negative word slips out, the other will say, "Do you believe we get to do this?"

It works almost every time! We immediately recognize our missteps, laugh, and repent of negative words. This discipline of "nipping negative words in the bud" is a priceless pearl.

I shudder to think where I would be today without my bride. She is my Holy Spirit helper, and, Lord knows, I need a lot of help.

Do you have a Holy Spirit helper? Ask, and you will receive. Seek, and you will find someone you can hold yourself accountable to in the area of your speech. If you do, you will be blessed.

If you are married to a Christian spouse, you already have a Holy Spirit helper. You simply need to recognize the gift God has given you and make the decision and commitment to hold yourself accountable to them with your words.

If you are single, pray and ask the Lord to help you recognize a mature Christian in your close circle of friends or a family member who may become your accountability partner.

My dad had a poem by Walter Wintle mounted on the wall over his desk for many years. It is entitled "The Man Who Thinks He Can."

To help illustrate my point about how powerful words are, I would like to exercise some poetic license and offer you the following paraphrase, which we can call "The Man Who Says He Can."

> If you say you're beaten, you are,
> If you say you dare not, you don't.

If you'd like to win but say you can't,
It's almost a cinch you won't.

If you say you'll lose, you're lost,
For in the world, you will find
Success begins with a fellow's words,
It's all in the state of mind.

Full many a race is lost
Ere ever a step is run.

And many a coward fails
Ere ever his work's begun.

Speak big, and your deeds will grow.

Speak small, and you'll fall behind.

Say you can, and you surely will,
It's all in the state of mind.

A paraphrase of this old poem works so well because there is such a dynamic relationship between our thoughts, words, and deeds. They are, in a sense, the Trinity of our human behavior.

The old Chinese philosopher, Lao Tzu, explained it this way:

> Watch your thoughts, they become your words; watch your words, they become your actions; watch your actions, they become your habits; watch your habits, they become your character, watch your character, it becomes your destiny.

Not to sound redundant, but, for me, the age-old debate between man's free will and the sovereignty of God is settled in Philippians 2:12–13.

Philippians 2:12 makes clear we must "work out" our salvation. Philippians 2:13 comforts us by reassuring us we are not alone in this quest. There, Paul reassures us that God is within us, willing and acting on our behalf.

God is for us! In Jeremiah 29:11, He reminds us He has plans for us. "'For I know the plans I have for you,' declares the Lord, 'plans to prosper you and not to harm you, plans to give you hope and a future.'"

If we are Spirit-born, God is within us. He works with us in our thoughts, helps us with our words and attitudes, and desires to be glorified through our actions and lifestyle.

Will we miss the mark from time to time? Of course, we will. That's why we need the Savior. That's why we need to yield, one day at a time (one hour at a time, one minute at a time) to the Holy Spirit. He is a friend that is closer than a brother.

Have you ever started to say something, and the Holy Spirit convicts you in mid-sentence? This is a good thing. When He does, don't even finish the sentence. Simply say out loud, "Ooops, I was about to say something that is better left unsaid," and move on.

If you never get convicted by the Holy Spirit about the words you hear coming out of your mouth, there is an old Jewish cure more powerful than Jewish penicillin (chicken soup). It is called repentance!

As Dr. Caroline Leaf reminds us, our mind has dominion over our brain. We are created with the ability to monitor our own thoughts, words, and deeds. God is calling each of us to walk circumspectly. Taking a regular inventory of our speech is an essential ingredient to a walk and lifestyle which pleases and glorifies God.

As Joyce Meyer says, "I may not be where I ought to be, but I'm not where I used to be." Progress, not perfection, is our battle cry in the war of words we are all engaged in.

As I bring *A Shepherd's Pearls* to a conclusion, I would like to illustrate the power words have with one more personal testimony.

As I shared earlier, my relationship with my dad was unique, as all relationships are.

Dad was a real man's man. He preferred a strong handshake rather than a hug. He wasn't cheap with his "atta boy," but, despite him possessing the most incredible vocabulary of anyone I have ever known, there were three words I never heard him say as I was growing up.

Dad would always sign my birthday cards in his trademark bold penmanship. With his red fountain pen loaded with Indian ink, he would write, "Heaps O Love" or "Love ya, Dad," but never said the words, "I love you."

Our relationship, strained through my parent's divorce, was further challenged by my leaving Dad to live with my mom when I was seventeen. For the next seven years, we had literally no communication with each other whatsoever.

This silence was broken by my grandfather's passing. At my grandpop's funeral, we exchanged a brief hello. This ice breaker was followed up with years of sporadic, often terse letters.

I remember summoning the courage to write Dad and request a $1,500 loan to help buy a car. Instead of the loan, I received a short sarcastic note suggesting I get a second job. He was right, of course. He usually was.

I did end up getting a second job, and by the grace of God and a lot of hard work, we were delivered from the land of extreme lack.

When I was thirty years old, Jean and I were at a place where we could afford to take our first real vacation. We decided to take our two adorable kids on a trip to Florida. As we were planning our trip, we scheduled a visit with Jean's sister, who lived in Central Florida. Visiting Dad in North Miami wasn't even on the table. However, after I was convicted by the Holy Spirit to "honor your father and mother," I suggested we plan a very brief overnight stay with Dad and my stepmother, Rosemarie. This way, Dad could see his amazing grandkids, and I could check off my "honor your father" mandate.

As our Florida vacation unfolded, we were, as we had so carefully planned, in Dad and Rosemarie's home for less than twenty-four hours. Our brief visit was cordial but formal. Our kids lit up the room and softened the strained conversations considerably. When it came time to say goodbye, I extended my hand, expecting to receive one of my dad's strong ceremonial handshakes. Much to my surprise, Dad pushed my hand away, hugged me, and said, "I love you, son."

Those four words healed something deep inside me. That was a defining moment in my life and the catalyst for an amazing paradigm shift in my relationship with my dad.

Our visits to North Miami were still more formal than what we would choose, but we visited frequently. I always looked forward to a big hug from Dad at our arrival and departure.

At the moment of his death, Dad kissed his ring that was on my finger and told my sisters and me...one more time, "I love you," and then he left us.

If you have received any pearl of wisdom or discovery from this scribble of mine, receive this. Words matter. Tell those you love, "I love you." It may change their life.

Jesus loves you, and so do I.

## Faith Challenge Question

- Who has encouraged you in your life?

- Who are you accountable to?

- Is your speech positive or negative?

- When has Holy Spirit convicted you?

- How often do you hear or say, I love you?

# The Pearl of Great Price

*"For God so loved the world" (John 3:16).*

It's not often I am up before the morning paper arrives, but this is no ordinary day. He's so young, only seventeen, and now a member of the United States Army. They said they'd come for him at 5 a.m. and that they did. Not 4:59, not 5:01, but 5 a.m. sharp. It was the appointed time. We knew it was coming. We know in our hearts it is for good, but that doesn't make it easy.

The house is painfully quiet right now. My son Jimmy is gone. He left just moments ago to go to a place called Fort Sill, Oklahoma, to begin basic combat training. Oh, how I will miss him. How I will miss the sound of his laugh, the flash of his smile, the smell of his aftershave as he whisks by on his way to a date. No doubt, the coming weeks and months will be filled with impromptu reminders of my son, my only son, whom I love so much. My memories will comfort me some. We had such good times on the golf course together. Wow, how that guy can hit a golf ball. And he was such a popular kid. I've never seen anyone with more friends than Jimmy. No wonder he made homecoming court two years in a row. Voted the vice-president of the senior class and best looking in the school: imagine that, my son, the best looking! He always did take after his mom.

*Our son, U.S. Army Specialist James A. Brissey, III*

When Jimmy was a boy, he loved baseball. He was an excellent catcher and a darned good shortstop. I'll never forget the big catch he made one year during the important playoff game to save his team from defeat or the time just a couple of years ago when he stole not only second and then third base but stole home plate also. He led his team in stolen bases. He was so quick, so agile, so full of life and promise. Where did all the years go?

God help him now to be strong. Comfort him when he feels so alone. Guard his heart as the drill sergeant makes sport of him. How it pricks my heart to think of that. He's on his own now. Daddy can't take his place this time. He must do it on his own. Help him not to quit when his body tells him to and to find hope when it eludes those around him. Help him, oh God, to know that he is not alone, for our prayers and our hearts are with him. Give Your angels charge over him and protect him from the evil one and from himself.

As Christians, we love to celebrate Christmas. Joy to the world! A Savior has come to demonstrate God's great love and save us from our sins. "For God so loved the world that he gave his one and only Son" (John 3:16). Every year around Christmas time, it seems the whole world is touched by special grace. Many times we see the effects of Christmas in the faces of those we encounter in the mall or across the dinner table. There is a glow that seems to overshadow the struggles of life. There is a richness of peace that seems to permeate the air. "For unto us a child is born, unto us a son is given" (Isaiah 9:6, KJV).

John the Beloved tells us in his Gospel, "In the beginning was the Word, and the Word was with God, and the Word was God" (John 1:1). And in John 1:14, God's Word says, "The word became flesh and made his dwelling among us." This morning, in the shadow of my son's departure, I more fully appreciate what God has done. Somehow, though in a small way, I have tasted a new part of God's plan and of His Christmas. How quiet heaven must have seemed to the Father as the world received its Christ, as our Lord and elder brother stepped from eternity's heaven to put on an earth-suit. How the Father's heart must have broken on that first Christmas morn. What a void Jesus must have left in heaven when the appointed time came. How strange it must have seemed for heaven to be without His laughter, and how dark it must have seemed without His smile. Oh, how it must have stabbed the Father's heart when the soldiers mocked and crucified His Son. "For God so loved ...he gave his one and only Son" (John 3:16). This indeed is love beyond mine. It is a love beyond understanding or finding out. "See what great love the Father has lavished on us, that we should be called children of God!" (1 John 3:1). Oh, Christian, let us not take this love lightly or allow it to be without effect. Great is the sacrifice of our heavenly Father! Mighty is the work of His only Son. This life indeed will have its troubles, but we must remember: He has overcome the world! In the hours ahead, my mind will undoubtedly be filled with baseball games and bicycle races, birthday parties and family vacations, Christmases, and special times with loved ones. Life is filled with change, and though change might be for good, it is not always easy. Lord, be with my son. Keep him safe from harm. Watch over him and protect him from his enemies and himself. Keep him in Your care and in Your will. Help him—and us—to live in such a way that we are mindful always of Your great love. Reassure our fearful hearts that You are love, and Your love never fails!

# BIBLIOGRAPHY

Hegstrom, Paul. *Broken Children, Grown-Up Pain.* Beacon Hill Press of Kansas City, 2006.

Manning, Brennan. *The Ragamuffin Gospel.* Multnomah Press, 2000.

Wilkerson, Gary. *David Wilkerson.* World Challenge, Inc., 2014.

Yancey, Philip. *What's So Amazing About Grace?* Zondervan, 1997.

Batterson, Mark. *In a Pit with a Lion on a Snowy Day.* Multnomah Press, 2016.

Foster, Richard J. *Celebration of Discipline.* HarperCollins, 1998.

Frangipane, Francis. *The Three Battlegrounds.* Arrow Publications, 1996.

Nair, Ken. *Discovering the Heart of a Man.* Thomas Nelson Publishers, 1995.

Bevere, John. *Honor's Reward.* Hachette Book Group, 2007.

Leaf, Caroline. *Switch on Your Brain.* Baker Books, 2015.

Howard-Browne, Rodney. *The Touch of God.* Word & Spirit Publishing, 1992.

Warren, Rick. *The Purpose Driven Life.* Zondervan, 2002.

Hayford, Jack. *Living the Spirit-Formed Life.* Chosen Books, 2017.

# ENDNOTES

[1] Frankl, Viktor E. Man's Search for Meaning. Washington Square Press, 1985.

# ABOUT THE AUTHOR:

Jim and Jean Brissey, married for 45 years, are Founding Pastors of Higher Ground Ministries in Deland, FL. They have spearheaded more than 1,000 outreaches over 25 years. Jim earned a Bachelor of Biblical Studies from Omega Bible Institute and Seminary. Jim also served as the Florida Director for the Billy Graham Evangelistic Association for three years. Jim and Jean continue to serve with their grown children who now pastor the local church.

**HIGHER GROUND School Of MINISTRY**

*Information... Impartation... Activation*

*hgsmedu.org*

*Higher Ground School of Ministry* is committed to providing quality ministry training and ministry credentials with information, impartation and activation.

- *Fully accredited*
- *Classes are available online*
- *Start any time, move at your own pace*
- *No binding contracts*
- *Anointed, relevant and affordable*

**www.highergroundministries.org**

Higher Ground Ministries
820 N. Frankfort Ave.
Deland, FL. 32724
Higherground_1@msn.com

## Other books authored by Jim Brissey:

"A Shepherd's Heart"

"Step 13: Do You Want to Get Well?"

Available at amazon.com

e-Books available at

**www.hgsmedu.org**

CPSIA information can be obtained
at www.ICGtesting.com
Printed in the USA
BVHW081630130722
641967BV00004B/9